THE *lemonade* COOKBOOK

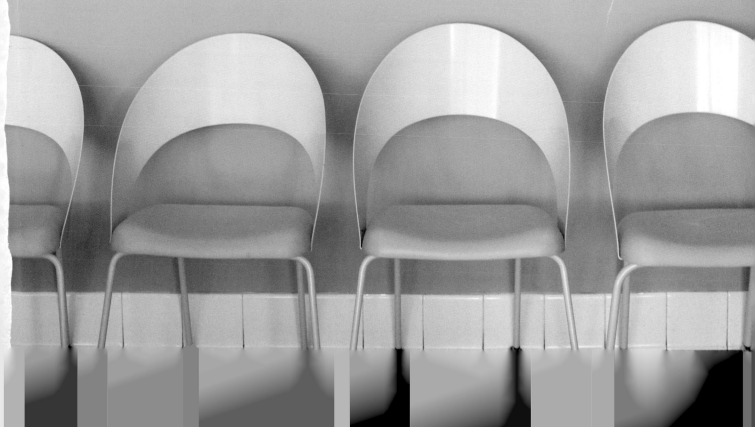

THE *lemonade* COOKBOOK

SOUTHERN CALIFORNIA COMFORT FOOD FROM L.A.'S FAVORITE MODERN CAFETERIA

ALAN JACKSON and **JOANN CIANCIULLI**

Photographs by Victoria Pearson

ST. MARTIN'S PRESS
NEW YORK

TO HEIDI, ADELINE, AMELIA, AND LUCKY

www.stmartins.com

Book design by Rita Sowins / Sowins Design
Production manager: Adriana Coada
Prop Styling by Jennifer Barquiarena

Library of Congress Cataloging-in-Publication Data Available Upon Request

ISBN 978-1-250-02366-7 (hardcover)
ISBN 978-1-4668-3866-6 (e-book)

St. Martin's Press books may be purchased for educational, business, or promotional use. For information on bulk purchases, please contact Macmillan Corporate and Premium Sales Department at 1-800-221-7945 extension 5442 or write specialmarkets@macmillan.com.

First Edition: October 2013

10   9   8   7

CONTENTS

INTRODUCTION

EVERYONE HAS HEARD OF CALIFORNIA CUISINE, BUT IS THERE SUCH A THING AS SOUTHERN CALIFORNIA CUISINE? YOU BET!

Los Angeles is one of the most vibrant cultural centers of the world, and after New York, the highest populated city in the nation. As such, the City of Angels boasts an eclectic and dynamic food scene in terms of range and depth.

The strength of this city's pulse is in its culinary identity, one that crosses many boundaries. Here expats from all nations melt into a custom blend of people, places, and diverse ideas. Cuisines of various lands have taken root in Los Angeles and there is no better window into a culture than through its food.

What defines L.A.'s food culture is its eclectic ethnic communities, Mediterranean climate, local farming, and the fact that it has one of the largest ports in the country with access to exotic produce, livestock, and spices from all over the world. Californians have always eaten things that other parts of the country didn't. As a child, I grew up eating artichokes and avocados that weren't common anywhere else in the U.S. until the 1980s. There's an innate, relaxed, and open way people on the West Coast communicate, travel, and eat.

The influence of California's increasingly ethnic cuisine has helped usher in a greater acceptance for international flavors across the country. Today, people are interested in powerful flavors and the American palate is more willing to try new things.

I was born and bred in Los Angeles and have been cooking here my entire life. After launching two of the city's most acclaimed fine-dining restaurants—Jackson's in Hollywood, and The Farm in Beverly Hills—followed by a successful catering company, I recognized there was something oddly missing in the industry, both in eating out and in my family life. Food of variety and substance does not necessarily entail the trappings of white tablecloths and valet parking. As a chef, I appreciate the fact that heavy, overwrought dishes have little place in today's diet, yet must be alive and interesting enough for people to actually enjoy eating.

So in 2007, I did a 180-degree flip and opened the first LEMONADE in West Hollywood. LEMONADE's cuisine is best described as Southern California comfort food served in a modern cafeteria setting. Now with multiple locations that span the city from Venice Beach to Downtown L.A., LEMONADE has become a citywide favorite in a city varied enough to put kimchi in a taco or smoked salmon on a pizza, LEMONADE's array of marketplace vegetables, unique sandwiches, and slow-simmered stews taste as though every culture stirred a bit into the pot.

"LOS ANGELES HAS IT ALL—IT'S CAR CULTURE AND COACHELLA, SURFERS AND YOGA MOMS, BEACHES AND CELEBRITIES, NWA AND THE RED HOT CHILI PEPPERS."

"LEMONADE HAS BECOME A CITYWIDE FAVORITE ... WHERE THE DISHES ARE AS CREATIVE AND DIVERSE AS L.A.'s INHABITANTS."

At its core, LEMONADE is a modern deli, with a rotating spread of marketplace vegetables as the focus instead of meat. To be clear, our food is vegetable-centric, not vegetarian. We feature plenty of hot dishes, many of them with animal protein. I like to think of our menu as a Southern California smorgasbord, where people are free to shape their own meals by mixing and matching dishes based on preference.

It's this contemporary and accessible approach that has made LEMONADE so popular and transitions perfectly to the home kitchen. There is something fun and adaptable about this way of flexible eating, both in dining out and cooking at home. Satisfying the everyday food gap for what's in the fridge, *The Lemonade Cookbook* is structured with the modern American cook in mind. Made to share, it gives everyone in your family freedom of choice and opens up endless meal options. Like a perfect-fit T-shirt, the scenario dictates the right size, whether you are visiting friends at a picnic or grabbing a single lunch to go on a busy day. For example, the *Skirt Steak*, *Balsamic Bermuda Onion*, *Poblano Pepper* (page 76) with its smoky depth, ping-pongs perfectly with snappy *Chinese Long Bean*, *Pluot Plum*, *Plum Vinaigrette* (page 42).

The Lemonade Cookbook speaks to a new generation of foodies who want sophisticated urban comfort food without it being outdated. The recipes are full of quick, flexible, all-purpose ideas, with plenty of suggestions for variations and embellishments. For instance, *Traditional Beef Short Rib* (page 109) performs double duty. Leftover short rib meat is cross-utilized and transformed into a succulent family favorite of *Beef Stronganoff* (page 114). With this user-friendly approach, the watchword is variation and the goal is inspiration.

Eating healthy sprinkled with a bit of sweet indulgence is very SoCal! Decadent desserts include tiny *Carrot Cupcakes* (page 198), giant *Oatmeal Golden Raisin Cookies* (page 189), and refreshing *Green Apple Jalapeño Lemonade* (page 234).

Recipes change like tastes change. It's the evolution of a confident cook to acknowledge this and adapt to suit your needs—nothing's written in stone, and what fun is cooking if you can't play with your food? Consider a recipe as a food GPS, a culinary road map that, once you navigate the intended route, can lead you to arrive at the original delicious destination. Even if you take a wrong turn, sometimes it's beneficial to get lost in order to find your own path. I hope you walk away from this book as a more confident and intuitive cook.

You don't have to live in L.A. to be a California cook. What you *do* need is an L.A. spirit of adventure about food, an appreciation of the freshest seasonal ingredients, and a desire to reinterpret familiar dishes with unexpected twists. LEMONADE was born in L.A., evoking the universal spirit of a bright sunny day in Southern California. This cookbook is real food for everyday life, no matter where you live.

MARKETPLACE VEGETABLES

EATING YOUR VEGETABLES SHOULDN'T FEEL LIKE PUNISHMENT. Lemonade has become famous for the freshness and originality of our menu, showcasing the abundance of seasonal vegetables in a fun and creative way. We do this by using bold flavors and daring colors to make the vegetables "cravable." At the center of every dish is the unadulterated vegetable, be it broccoli, avocado, or cabbage. The goal is to take that key ingredient and elaborate on it, while still keeping the vegetable at the heart of the final dish.

I call these dishes "Marketplace Vegetables" because I don't consider them traditional "salads" by any means. Think about it, when you order a typical salad isn't the lettuce just filler and it's really about the delicious yummy nibbles you inevitably dig for? Think chopped tomatoes, roasted red peppers, sharp cheeses, and toasted nuts. Here, we showcase those crunchy, chewy, satisfying elements on their own and ditch the greens altogether. With the exception of *Arugula, Fig, Blue Cheese* (page 29), none of our Marketplace Vegetables include greens or lettuce, and even in that recipe, the arugula acts more as the garnish for fruity figs and pungent blue cheese.

The thing to remember is that all of the Marketplace dishes complement one another, some are completely vegetarian, and others have grains and animal protein (see the next two chapters). When served together, these dishes are an enjoyable vegetable medley of varying tastes and textures that impress dinner guests with a meatless meal worth bragging about.

BEET, PICKLED RED ONION, HAZELNUT VINAIGRETTE

MAKES 4 CUPS

There is an ethnic stretch of Eastern-European bakeries and delis on Santa Monica Boulevard in the Fairfax district of L.A. The colorful display of pickled foods they offer is staggering—cabbage, cucumbers, and beets just to name a few. As a kid, my mother, Alana, would often bring home a pungent vinegar-infused Russian vegetable dish, chock-full of beets, onions, and dill, and coated in tangy sour cream. Here, the nutty richness of hazelnuts replaces sour cream to create a modern-casual adaptation.

1 pound red beets (about 3 medium), tops trimmed
1 cup Pickled Red Onion, coarsely chopped (recipe follows)
½ cup blanched hazelnuts, toasted and coarsely chopped
¼ cup Hazelnut Vinaigrette (recipe follows)
Coarse salt and freshly ground black pepper

TOASTING NUTS

Preheat the oven to 325 degrees F. Spread the nuts out in a single layer on a rimmed baking pan. Bake, checking the nuts and shaking the pan every few minutes, until they are fragrant and lightly toasted; this should take anywhere from 8 to 12 minutes, depending on the type of nut. For example, pine nuts toast faster than walnuts.

BRING A LARGE POT OF SALTED WATER TO BOIL. Submerge the beets, cover the pot, reduce the heat to low, and simmer for 25 to 30 minutes. To check for doneness, insert a paring knife into the center of the beets; it should slide in without any resistance.

DRAIN THE BEETS IN A COLANDER and when cool enough to handle, rub the skins off with paper towels or an old dish towel. Set the beets aside in the refrigerator to chill. The beets can easily be prepared in advance, covered, and refrigerated.

WHEN THE BEETS ARE CHILLED, cut them in a small dice and put into a mixing bowl. Warning! You may want to wear rubber gloves and put a piece of wax paper on your cutting board so you don't stain everything red!

TO THE BEETS, ADD THE PICKLED ONIONS, hazelnuts, and vinaigrette. Season with salt and pepper; toss thoroughly to combine.

PICKLED RED ONION

This indispensable condiment adds the perfect crunch, tang, and snap to burgers, sandwiches, and tacos.

1 cup Champagne vinegar
1 cup water
¼ cup sugar
1 tablespoon pickling spice
1 large red onion, halved lengthwise
   and thinly sliced

COMBINE THE VINEGAR, WATER, SUGAR, AND PICKLING SPICE IN A MEDIUM POT. Slowly bring to a simmer over medium-low heat, stirring occasionally to dissolve the sugar. Put the onions in a heatproof container, pour the hot liquid on top, and toss to coat evenly; the onions should be completely submerged in the liquid.

COVER AND COOL TO ROOM TEMPERATURE. The longer the onions steep the better; shoot for at least 2 hours. Chill before serving. The pickled onions keep for months stored covered in the refrigerator. Be sure to keep them completely submerged in the brine.

Makes about 2 cups

HAZELNUT VINAIGRETTE

When making the hazelnut oil for the base of this vinaigrette, it's important to take the time to lightly toast the hazelnuts to bring out their innate nuttiness, and then immediately blend the nuts with the oil while they're still warm. The residual heat provokes the hazelnuts to release their essential oils and infuse the vinaigrette with flavor.

HAZELNUT OIL
¼ cup blanched hazelnuts, toasted
   (see page 3)
⅔ cup canola oil

VINAIGRETTE
¼ cup sherry vinegar
2 tablespoons honey or agave nectar
1 teaspoon freshly squeezed lemon
   juice
1 teaspoon orange juice
½ small shallot, minced
1 teaspoon coarse salt
¼ teaspoon freshly ground black
   pepper
⅔ cup hazelnut oil (from above)

TO PREPARE THE HAZELNUT OIL, combine the nuts and oil in a blender. Blend at high speed for about 1 minute or until the nuts are completely broken down and incorporated into the oil. Pour into a jar or container and set aside. As the oil sits, the ground nuts will settle to the bottom.

TO PREPARE THE VINAIGRETTE, in a mixing bowl combine the vinegar, honey, lemon and orange juices, shallot, salt and pepper. Gently blend with a whisk.

ONCE THE BASE INGREDIENTS ARE COMBINED, pour in the hazelnut oil along with all of the ground nut "goop." Lightly whisk until the ingredients just come together; this is not an emulsified vinaigrette. Pour the vinaigrette into a plastic container or jar and shake it up just before you are ready to dress the vegetables. Keep any leftover vinaigrette covered in the refrigerator for up to 1 week.

Makes 1 cup

BRUSSELS SPROUT, SHAVED PARMESAN, SHERRY VINAIGRETTE

MAKES 4 CUPS

Brussels sprouts are on the top of many peoples' most hated vegetable list because when they're boiled to death and overcooked, the result is a mushy and bitter mess. A different beast entirely, this golden-crusted version has the ability to turn even the most vigilant Brussels sprout–haters around to the other side. Delicate and hearty at the same time, these badass baby cabbages are terrific served either hot or cold. If serving hot for a holiday dinner, skip adding the vinaigrette after roasting, and simply toss with shaved Parmesan and a couple of knobs of butter.

1½ pounds Brussels sprouts, ends trimmed, yellow outer leaves discarded
1 cup Sherry Vinaigrette (see page 29)
Coarse salt
Freshly ground black pepper
1 cup shaved Parmesan cheese (about 2 ounces)

PREHEAT THE OVEN TO 350 DEGREES F. Bring a large pot of salted water to a boil over high heat.

HALVE THE BRUSSELS SPROUTS LENGTHWISE and add them to the boiling water. Par-cook for 2 minutes until softened slightly. Drain the sprouts in a colander and transfer to a mixing bowl.

While the sprouts are still warm, toss with ¼ cup of the vinaigrette to coat. Because the sprouts are still warm, they really absorb the vinaigrette and soak up the flavor.

TRANSFER THE SPROUTS TO A LARGE BAKING PAN and spread them out into a single layer. Season generously with salt and pepper. Roast the Brussels sprouts for 25 minutes, until slightly charred on the outside and tender on the inside; shake the pan from time to time to brown the sprouts evenly.

Put the sprouts into a bowl and allow to cool to room temperature. The Brussels sprouts can easily be prepared in advance, covered, and refrigerated.

TO THE COOLED ROASTED BRUSSELS SPROUTS, add the remaining ¾ cup of vinaigrette, cheese, and season with salt and pepper.

CAULIFLOWER, GOLDEN RAISIN, ALMOND, CURRY VINAIGRETTE

MAKES 4 CUPS

Cauliflower can be a little bland on its own, but blasting the florets in a hot oven concentrates its natural sweetness and makes the lily-white vegetable transformed to a crisp caramel brown. Tossing the roasted cauliflower with Curry Vinaigrette brightens the charred flavor. This is a universal side that goes especially well with Harissa Chicken (page 89), or lamb chops; or for a complete meal, toss with shredded rotisserie chicken from the deli counter.

1 head cauliflower (about 2 pounds),
    cut into florets
¼ cup olive oil
Coarse salt and freshly ground black
    pepper
1 cup whole almonds, toasted
    (see page 3)
¼ cup golden raisins
½ cup Curry Vinaigrette
    (recipe follows)

PREHEAT THE OVEN TO 400 DEGREES F.

PUT THE CAULIFLOWER ON A LARGE BAKING PAN, drizzle with the oil, toss to coat, and spread out in a single layer. Season generously with salt and pepper. Roast for 25 to 30 minutes until tender and slightly charred, shaking the pan from time to time. Put the roasted cauliflower in a mixing bowl; add the almonds and raisins. Toss with the curry vinaigrette to evenly coat. May be served warm, cold, or at room temperature.

CURRY VINAIGRETTE

This dynamite Curry Vinaigrette starts with making a flavorful curry oil, which can also be used for sautéing scallops or frying potatoes. The robust vinaigrette will make more than you need for the roasted cauliflower, which is a good thing. Drizzle on a flaky piece of grilled halibut or use as a dip for toasted pita bread.

1 cup canola oil, plus 2 tablespoons
1 Granny Smith apple, halved
    lengthwise, cored, and coarsely
    chopped
1 small onion, coarsely chopped
2 tablespoons turmeric
1 tablespoon curry powder,
    preferably Madras

VINAIGRETTE
1 tablespoon whole-grain Dijon
    mustard
1 tablespoon honey or agave nectar
2 tablespoons apple cider vinegar
Juice of ½ lemon
1 tablespoon orange juice
Coarse salt and freshly ground black
    pepper

CORING AN APPLE

Cut the apple in half lengthwise, from top to bottom. Simply remove the core with the help of a melon baller or teaspoon, giving it a quick twist around the seeds to scoop them out. Cut off the stem and bud end of the apple with a knife. Then slice the apple as directed in the recipe.

TO PREPARE THE CURRY OIL, put a small pot over medium-low heat and coat with 2 tablespoons of the canola oil. When the oil is hot, add the apple and onion. Cook and stir until soft and fragrant, 2 to 3 minutes. Stir in the turmeric and curry, and cook until the spices begin to darken slightly, about 1 minute, taking care not to allow the spices to burn.

POUR IN THE REMAINING 1 CUP OF OIL and stir everything together. Increase the heat to medium and bring the oil to a boil. Boil for 1 minute, then remove the oil from the heat and allow to cool to room temperature. Strain the oil into a container to discard the pieces of apple and onion. Let the curry powder settle to the bottom of the container. To keep the oil clear, try not to disturb the curry sediment.

TO PREPARE THE VINAIGRETTE, in a mixing bowl combine the mustard, honey, vinegar, lemon, and orange juices. Gently blend with a whisk; season with salt and pepper. Pour in the oil, taking care not to disturb the curry sediment settled at the bottom, and lightly whisk until the ingredients just come together; this is not an emulsified vinaigrette.

POUR THE VINAIGRETTE into a plastic container or jar and shake it up just before you are ready to dress the vegetables. Keep any leftover vinaigrette covered in the refrigerator for up to 1 week.

Makes 1 cup

BROCCOLI, RICOTTA,
CHAMPAGNE VINAIGRETTE

MAKES 4 CUPS

When fresh broccoli is roasted like it is here, the florets char slightly and take on a wonderful, earthy flavor. The Champagne Vinaigrette has an elegant floral sweetness, which elevates a seemingly basic broccoli dish to something out of the ordinary.

2 heads broccoli (about 2 pounds),
    cut into florets
¼ cup olive oil
Coarse salt and freshly ground black
    pepper
⅓ cup grated ricotta salata
½ cup Champagne Vinaigrette
    (recipe follows)

RICOTTA SALATA

Ricotta salata is a hard cheese with a mildly salty, nutty, and milky flavor. Ricotta Salata is typically made from sheep's milk, and has a distinctive, snowy white color, which stands out strikingly against vivid hues like emerald-colored broccoli.

PREHEAT THE OVEN TO 400 DEGREES F.

PUT THE BROCCOLI ON A LARGE BAKING PAN, drizzle with the oil, toss to coat and spread out in a single layer. Season generously with salt and pepper. Roast, shaking the pan from time to time, until tender and slightly charred, 20 to 25 minutes. Transfer the roasted broccoli to a mixing bowl and set aside to cool. The broccoli can easily be prepared in advance, covered, and refrigerated.

TO THE COOLED ROASTED BROCCOLI, add the cheese and vinaigrette; season with salt and pepper. Toss well to combine. Served chilled or at room temperature.

RAW EGG

The FDA suggests caution in consuming raw eggs due to the slight risk of salmonella or other food borne illness. To reduce this risk, I recommend you use only fresh, clean, properly refrigerated, grade A or AA, preferably organic eggs with intact shells, and avoid contact between the yolks or whites and the shell.

CHAMPAGNE VINAIGRETTE

A universal Champagne Vinaigrette should always be on the refrigerator door. Good on just about everything, drizzle on vegetables that are low in acidity, such as avocado, zucchini, kale, and broccoli. The Champagne Vinaigrette has the right amount of acidity and sweetness to complement these vegetables.

1 large egg yolk
1 teaspoon Dijon mustard
1 teaspoon honey or agave nectar
2 tablespoons Champagne vinegar
½ teaspoon coarse salt
¼ teaspoon freshly ground black pepper
¾ cup canola oil
½ small shallot, minced

IN A BLENDER, combine the egg yolk, mustard, honey, vinegar, salt, and pepper. Blend on medium speed for a few seconds, and then reduce the speed to low. With the motor running, slowly add the oil until emulsified. Pour into a container or jar and mix in the shallot. Keep any leftover vinaigrette covered in the refrigerator for up to 2 days.

Makes 1 cup

GREEN TOMATO, SWEET CORN, PEPITA, AND ANCHO CHILI VINAIGRETTE

MAKES 4 CUPS

It may sound odd, but fresh corn is so much better unadulterated and cut straight off the cob! Here, the small sweet kernels are tossed with tart tomatoes, crunchy pepitas, and smoky Ancho Chili Vinaigrette; perfect for a backyard barbecue. For a little more gusto, add grilled shrimp or black beans to make this vegetable dish more substantial or serve as a piccalilli relish to crown succulent crab cakes.

3 ears fresh corn, shucked, kernels cut
  from cob (about 2 cups)
2 medium Green Zebra tomatoes,
  cored and chopped (about 2 cups)
¼ cup pepitas (pumpkin seeds),
  toasted (see page 3)
½ cup coarsely chopped fresh
  cilantro
½ cup crumbled cotija cheese,
  (optional) (about 2 ounces)
½ cup Ancho Chili Vinaigrette
  (recipe follows)
½ teaspoon coarse salt
¼ teaspoon freshly ground black
  pepper

IN A LARGE BOWL, combine the corn, tomatoes, pepitas, cilantro, and cheese, if using. Pour the vinaigrette over the vegetables, season with salt and pepper, and toss to combine. Serve chilled or at room temperature.

GREEN TOMATOES

I prefer Green Zebra tomatoes (which have telltale streaky green-and-white skins) for their slightly tart taste. Truth is, almost any firm green tomato will do the trick. Actually, if you're jonesing for this fresh vegetable dish before green tomatoes show up at your market, simply swap in whichever red or other more vibrantly hued variety you prefer.

ANCHO CHILI VINAIGRETTE

Ancho is a sweet dried chili that imbibes a seductive, smoky depth. I love that it possesses full flavor but won't blow your head off with fiery spice. The coffee-colored Ancho Chili Vinaigrette also works as a marinade for Latin American-flavored grilled flank steak or drizzled on sweet tropical fruit, such as mango and papaya.

1 tablespoon ancho chili powder
1 chipotle pepper in adobo,
    seeded if desired and minced
1 jalapeño, halved, seeded, and
    minced
2 garlic cloves, minced
1 teaspoon ground cumin
¼ cup Champagne vinegar
Juice of 1 lime
1 tablespoon honey or agave nectar
1 cup canola oil
1 teaspoon coarse salt

IN A BLENDER, combine the ancho powder, chipotle, jalapeño, garlic, cumin, vinegar, lime juice, and honey. Blend until smooth. With the motor running, slowly add the oil until emulsified. Season with salt. Pour the vinaigrette into a plastic container or jar and keep any leftover covered in the refrigerator for up to 1 week.

Makes 1 cup

ANCHO CHILI POWDER

Finding pre-ground ancho chili powder should not be a problem for most people in the U.S. However, do not get it confused with "ground chile powder," which often is a mish-mash spice blend.

If you are inclined to make your own, you'll find anchos in a big clear plastic bag, usually in the ethnic foods aisle. Now that you've got anchos, making ancho chili powder is only a few steps away....

Remove the stems from as many anchos as you would like to make chili powder from. Do not remove the seeds, just the membrane that holds them—it should all come out with a good pull.

Cut the peppers into chunks. Working in batches, toss them in a *clean* coffee/spice grinder and give them a few really good spins while shaking the grinder, until the chili becomes a fine powder. Keep the ancho chili powder in a covered container, in a cupboard away from the stove, for up to 3 months.

HEIRLOOM TOMATO,
CRUSHED BASIL, FLEUR DE SEL

MAKES 4 CUPS

While you can easily prepare the components ahead of time, it's best to toss the ingredients together as close to when you're serving them as possible so they stay perky.

1½ pounds assorted ripe heirloom tomatoes such as brandywine, sungold, and red beefsteak
½ cup Basil Vinaigrette (recipe follows)
½ cup fresh basil leaves, hand torn
¼ teaspoon freshly ground black pepper
1 teaspoon fleur de sel

CUT THE BIGGER TOMATOES INTO ¼-INCH-THICK SLICES and quarter or halve the smaller ones; this vegetable salad looks great with different colored tomatoes of varying sizes and shapes. Put the tomatoes in a mixing bowl and pour in the vinaigrette. Toss gently, taking care not to smash the tomatoes. Sprinkle in the basil leaves. Season with pepper, and toss again to combine. When ready to serve, sprinkle with fleur de sel. Serve at room temperature. *Please* never, ever refrigerate tomatoes!

TOMATOES

When buying tomatoes look for those with intense color that feel firm and heavy, and smell like the plant itself. An underripe tomato can ripen on the kitchen counter at room temperature.

BASIL VINAIGRETTE

This stripped-down pesto eliminates the cheese, garlic, and pine nuts to create a dressing that's less assertive. Fresh parsley adds a grassy flavor while also keeping the dressing a deep emerald color. This herbal vinaigrette doubles as an uncooked sauce; try it on grilled firm fish like halibut or sea bass.

1½ cups fresh basil leaves, coarsely chopped
¼ cup fresh flat-leaf parsley, coarsely chopped
Juice of ½ lemon
¾ cup canola oil
1 teaspoon coarse salt
½ teaspoon fresh ground black pepper

IN A BLENDER, combine the basil, parsley, lemon juice, oil, salt and pepper. Blend on high speed for about 1 minute until smooth and green. Pour the vinaigrette into a container and keep any leftover covered in the refrigerator for up to 5 days.

Makes 1 cup

AVOCADO, CHERRY TOMATO, PINE NUT, LIME VINAIGRETTE

MAKES 4 CUPS

One of Lemonade's most beloved dishes, this simply delicious vegetable side places avocados front and center. Avocados are Mother Nature's butter, packed with good fat, fiber, and a whole host of vital vitamins and minerals. Plus, their smooth, creamy texture and earthy flavor allow them to shine in just about everything. The key here is to cut the avocados into large chunks and not mash the pieces like guacamole, so you can sink your teeth into the supple, silky flesh.

4 firm-ripe Hass avocados, halved, pitted, peeled, and cut into chunks
1 pint cherry or grape tomatoes, halved crosswise
¼ cup pine nuts, toasted (see page 3)
¼ cup Lime Vinaigrette (recipe follows)
Coarse salt and freshly ground black pepper

IN A MIXING BOWL, combine the avocados, tomatoes, pine nuts, and vinaigrette. Toss gently, taking care not to smash the pieces of avocado—you are not making guacamole! Season generously with salt and pepper. Serve chilled.

LIME VINAIGRETTE

A sweet, tangy blend of lime, honey, and cilantro, this versatile Lime Vinaigrette lends pizzazz to a Southwestern-style salad, or makes a great basic marinade for fish or chicken.

Juice of 2 to 3 limes, (about ¼ cup)
1 tablespoon honey or agave nectar
1 teaspoon Dijon mustard
1 garlic clove, minced
1 teaspoon coarse salt
1 teaspoon freshly ground black pepper
⅔ cup canola oil
3 tablespoons chopped fresh cilantro leaves

IN A BLENDER, combine the lime juice, honey, mustard, garlic, salt, and pepper. Blend on medium speed for a few seconds, and then reduce the speed to low. With the motor running, slowly add the oil until emulsified. Pour into a container or jar and mix in the cilantro. Keep any leftover vinaigrette covered in the refrigerator for up to 1 week.

Makes 1 cup

CELERY ROOT, WALNUT, CRÈME FRAÎCHE

MAKES 4 CUPS

Celery root, also called celeriac, is a curious unattractive fall/winter root vegetable that can be prepared many ways. The bistro dish, celery root rémoulade, is a classic, melding shaved raw celery root with creamy caper-mayonnaise dressing. If you've been passing over this vegetable just because of its gnarly appearance, quickly pop one or two in your cart on your next shopping trip. Celery root has a woodsy, celerylike flavor, but is far more concentrated and less watery than celery itself. In this recipe, soft raisins, crunchy walnuts, and tart crème fraîche elevate the dense, crisp texture of this underappreciated vegetable.

1 celery root (about 1½ pounds)
4 celery stalks, chopped
½ cup walnut pieces, toasted (see page 3)
½ cup dried currants or raisins
½ cup chopped fresh flat-leaf parsley
½ cup Sherry Vinaigrette (see page 29)
½ cup crème fraîche, sour cream, or plain nonfat Greek yogurt
1 teaspoon coarse salt
½ teaspoon freshly ground black pepper

IN A MIXING BOWL, combine the celery root, celery, walnuts, currants, and parsley. Add the vinaigrette, crème fraîche, salt, and pepper. Toss the slaw until the ingredients are well blended. Feel free to make the slaw an hour or two in advance; the flavor gets better as it sits. Serve chilled.

CELERY ROOT

Celery root needs to be peeled—and be aggressive when you do it. Don't even try to use a vegetable peeler, which will probably just break. Use a sharp chef's knife to lop off the bumps and knobby roots at the bottom. You can cut the remaining bulb in half so it's more manageable, then use a knife to take the thick skin off each half. Thinly slice the celery root into matchsticks by hand, with a mandolin, a food processor with a shredder blade, or grate with a box grater.

SWEET POTATO,
PARSLEY, PISTACHIO VINAIGRETTE

MAKES 4 CUPS

Whether sweet potatoes only enter your kitchen on Thanksgiving or have a regular spot in your cooking rotation, you could probably use more delicious ways to prepare them. This is a wonderfully aromatic dish with textures that range from silky-soft to faintly crunchy. Roasted sweet potatoes support hearty main dishes like braised Turkey, Dried Cranberry, Sage Gravy (page 124) and BBQ Brisket (page 110). Though this side starch is best at room temperature, it's also terrific served hot for your holiday table.

1 pound sweet potatoes (about 2 medium), unpeeled, scrubbed, and cut into 1-inch chunks
¼ cup olive oil
Coarse salt and freshly ground black pepper
⅓ cup Pistachio Vinaigrette (recipe follows)
⅓ cup shelled pistachios, toasted and crushed (see page 3)
½ cup chopped fresh flat-leaf parsley

PREHEAT THE OVEN TO 400 DEGREES F.

PUT THE SWEET POTATOES ON A LARGE BAKING PAN, drizzle with the oil, toss to coat, and spread out in a single layer. Season generously with salt and pepper. Roast, turning occasionally, until the potatoes begin to brown on corners and are just tender inside, 30 to 40 minutes. Transfer the roasted sweet potatoes to a mixing bowl and set aside to cool. The potatoes can easily be prepared in advance, covered, and refrigerated.

TO THE COOLED POTATOES, add the vinaigrette, pistachios, and parsley. Toss well to combine. Season with salt and pepper.

PISTACHIO VINAIGRETTE

The unique part about making this Pistachio Vinaigrette is bringing out the addictive character of the pistachios in a single taste. Extracting the nut oils through careful toasting and blending while warm is the trick. Keeping the nut "goop" in this dressing is important to add texture to the final product.

PISTACHIO OIL
¼ cup shelled pistachios, toasted
   (see page 3)
⅔ cup canola oil

VINAIGRETTE
2 tablespoons sherry vinegar
1 teaspoon lemon juice
1 teaspoon orange juice
1 tablespoon honey or agave nectar
½ small shallot, minced
½ teaspoon coarse salt
½ teaspoon freshly ground black
   pepper
¾ cup pistachio oil (from above)

TO PREPARE THE PISTACHIO OIL, combine the warm nuts and oil in a blender. Blend at high speed for about 1 minute or until the nuts are completely broken down and incorporated into the oil. Pour into a jar or container and set aside. As the oil sits, the ground nuts will settle to the bottom.

TO PREPARE THE VINAIGRETTE, in a mixing bowl combine the vinegar, honey, lemon and orange juices, shallot, salt and pepper. Gently blend with a whisk. Pour in the pistachio oil along with the nut goop all at once and lightly whisk until the ingredients just come together; this is not an emulsified vinaigrette. Pour into a plastic container or jar and shake it up just before you are ready to dress the dish. Keep any leftover vinaigrette covered in the refrigerator for up to 1 week.

Makes 1 cup

FINGERLING POTATO,
DILL, LEMON-SAFFRON VINAIGRETTE

MAKES 4 CUPS

Modeled after the French mayonnaise mix, this savory Provençal potato dish is welcomed at any picnic or paired with a piece of Citrus-Poached Salmon (page 99) and a glass of rosé.

2 pounds (about 24) fingerling
    potatoes, scrubbed
¼ cup olive oil
Coarse salt and freshly ground
    black pepper
½ cup Lemon-Saffron Vinaigrette
    (recipe follows)
½ cup crème fraîche, sour cream,
    or plain nonfat Greek yogurt
2 tablespoons coarsely chopped
    fresh dill
1 large shallot, thinly sliced

PREHEAT THE OVEN TO 400 DEGREES F.

PUT THE FINGERLING POTATOES ON A LARGE BAKING PAN, drizzle with the oil, toss to coat, and spread out in a single layer. Season generously with salt and pepper. Roast, shaking the pan from time to time, until they are golden on the outside and tender when pierced with a sharp knife, 25 to 30 minutes. Set the roasted potatoes aside to cool. The potatoes can easily be prepared in advance, covered, and refrigerated.

SLICE THE FINGERLING POTATOES CROSSWISE into ½-inch-thick pieces and put into a mixing bowl. Add the vinaigrette, crème fraîche, dill, and shallot. Toss to evenly combine the ingredients. Season with salt and pepper. Serve room temperature, chilled, or warm.

LEMON-SAFFRON VINAIGRETTE

Saffron is one of those coveted ingredients that merit high reverence in my kitchen. While the high cost per ounce adds a bit of mystique to the spice, thankfully a little goes a long way. In order to release saffron's unique aroma and flavor, you must steep the wiry red threads first. The result is a potent liquid with a golden hue that makes this vinaigrette not only gorgeous to look at but exotic tasting.

Large pinch of saffron threads
2 tablespoons hot water
1 large egg yolk (see page 10)
1 teaspoon Dijon mustard
Juice of 1 lemon, plus more if needed
½ teaspoon turmeric
1 teaspoon coarse salt
½ teaspoon freshly ground black
    pepper
¾ cup extra-virgin olive oil

IN A SMALL BOWL, combine the saffron with hot water. Stir to combine. Allow it to sit for a couple of minutes to bleed out the saffron's yellow color.

IN A BLENDER, combine the egg yolk, mustard, lemon, turmeric, saffron (along with the water), salt, and pepper. Blend on medium speed for a few seconds, and then reduce the speed to low. With the motor running, slowly add the oil until emulsified. Stir in 1 tablespoon of water or lemon juice to thin out if needed. Cover and refrigerate until ready to use. Keep any leftover vinaigrette covered in the refrigerator for up to 3 days.

Makes 1 cup

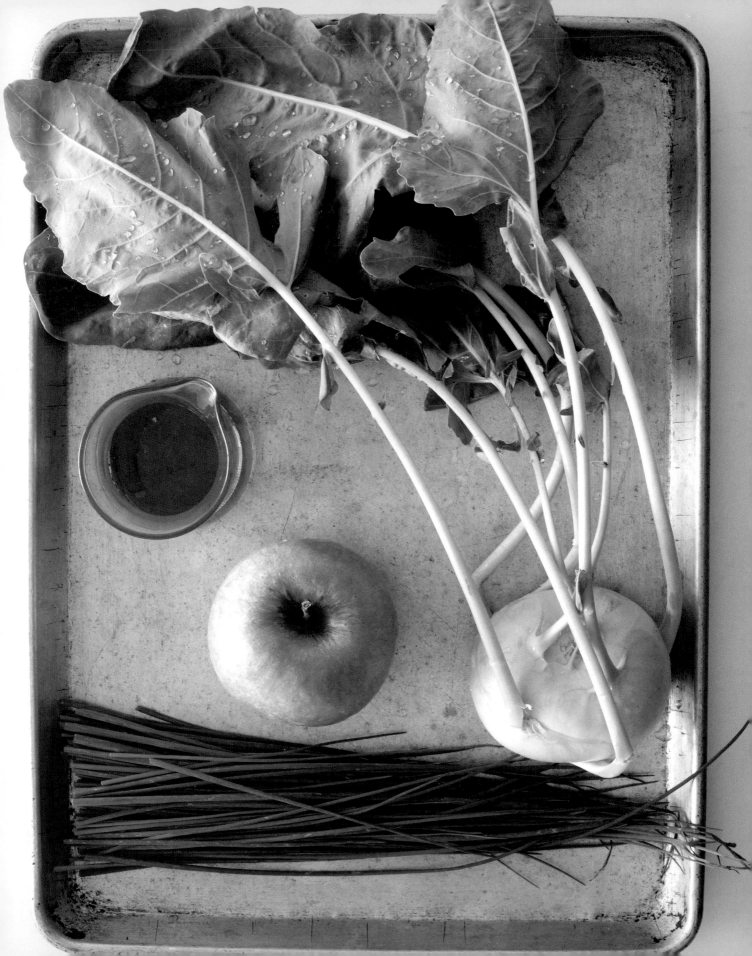

KOHLRABI, GRANNY SMITH APPLE, CHIVE, SESAME OIL

MAKES 4 CUPS

There are times when a food combination happens by mistake, much like the old-school "Reese's" commercials where a roller skater, eating chocolate, bumps into a guy eating peanut butter. Here, funky sesame oil works as an unexpected dressing to coat the crisp components of earthy kohlrabi and tart green apple.

1 kohlrabi (about ½ pound)
1 Granny Smith apple, halved
   lengthwise and cored
   (see page 9)
½ cup chopped fresh chives
2 tablespoons sesame oil
1 teaspoon coarse salt
½ teaspoon freshly ground black
   pepper

TO PREPARE THE KOHLRABI, snip off the leaf stems, then using a sharp knife, trim off the base and the antennae-like shoots on the top.

SET THE FLAT SIDE OF THE KOHLRABI on the cutting board. You can cut the bulb in half so it's more manageable, then take the thick skin off each half. Thinly slice the kohlrabi bulb into matchsticks by hand, with a mandolin, or grate with a box grater. Do the same with the apple, cutting it about the same size as the kohlrabi.

IN A MIXING BOWL, combine the kohlrabi, apple, chives, sesame oil, and salt and pepper. Toss the slaw until the ingredients are well blended. Feel free to make the slaw 1 to 2 hours in advance; the flavor gets better as it sits. Serve chilled.

KOHLRABI

Kolhrabi may look a little intimidating at first glance, but the freaky looking veggie is fairly easy to prepare. Kohlrabi is part of the cabbage family. The name translates as "turnip cabbage" and the mild, sweet flavor is somewhere between a turnip and a water chestnut, with a crunchy texture. It can be found in two colors, pale green and purple. When raw, kohlrabi is slightly crunchy and mildly spicy, like radishes. While it's available year-round, kohlrabi really peaks in the colder months.

ROASTED PARSNIP, PECORINO, VIDALIA ONION-BACON VINAIGRETTE

MAKES 4 CUPS

This unassuming roasted vegetable dish is so stellar, it is as much a main attraction as a side component. A festive mixture of colors and textures, the golden Roasted Parsnips really shine, retaining their characteristic earthiness while absorbing the salty smack of shredded pecorino and smoky bacon.

2 pounds parsnips (about 8 large), peeled, halved lengthwise, and sliced
2 tablespoons olive oil
Coarse salt and freshly ground black pepper
½ cup Vidalia Onion-Bacon Vinaigrette (recipe follows)
½ cup shaved pecorino cheese (about 1 ounce)
¼ cup chopped fresh flat-leaf parsley

PREHEAT THE OVEN TO 400 DEGREES F.

PUT THE PARSNIPS ON A LARGE BAKING PAN, drizzle with the oil, toss to coat and spread out in a single layer. Season generously with salt and pepper. Roast, shaking the pan from time to time, until just tender and slightly browned, 15 to 20 minutes. Allow the parsnips to cool to room temperature.

TRANSFER THE COOLED PARSNIPS to a mixing bowl. Toss with the vinaigrette, cheese, and parsley.

VIDALIA ONION–BACON VINAIGRETTE

Part compote and part relish, this chunky Vidalia Onion-Bacon Vinaigrette is absolutely addictive. The balanced flavor fires on all cylinders to hit the right notes of tart, smoky, and sweet. Try it as a dressing for a sandwich slaw or as a topper for crostini or fried eggs in the morning.

6 strips smoked bacon, cooked and chopped

1 small Vidalia onion, diced small

1 small Granny Smith apple, cored and diced small (see page 9)

2 tablespoons honey or agave nectar

2 tablespoons chopped fresh flat-leaf parsley

1 tablespoon sherry vinegar

1 teaspoon granulated garlic

¼ teaspoon dry mustard

1 teaspoon coarse salt

½ teaspoon freshly ground black pepper

¼ cup extra-virgin olive oil

TO PREPARE THE VINAIGRETTE, in a mixing bowl combine the bacon, onion, apple, honey, parsley, vinegar, garlic, mustard, salt, and pepper. Gently blend with a whisk. Pour in the oil all at once and lightly whisk until the ingredients just come together; this is not an emulsified vinaigrette. Pour into a plastic container or jar and shake it up just before you are ready to dress the vegetables. Keep any leftover vinaigrette covered in the refrigerator for up to 1 week.

Makes about 2 cups

ARUGULA, FIG, BLUE CHEESE,
SHERRY VINAIGRETTE

MAKES 4 CUPS

Sweet figs, sharp blue cheese, and peppery arugula make for a colorful and refreshing main or side salad bursting with flavor. Great for hot evenings in the summer! If fresh figs aren't available, rotate seasonal fruits like Asian pears or strawberries.

10 ounces baby arugula leaves

8 fresh Mission figs, stemmed, halved, and sliced crosswise (about 2 cups sliced)

2 ounces blue cheese, crumbled into medium-size chunks (about ⅓ cup)

⅓ cup Sherry Vinaigrette (recipe follows)

½ teaspoon coarse salt

¼ teaspoon freshly ground black pepper

IN A MIXING BOWL, combine the arugula, figs, and cheese. Drizzle with the vinaigrette, season with salt and pepper. Toss the ingredients together to lightly to coat.

SHERRY VINAIGRETTE

This Sherry Vinaigrette is a go-to multipurpose dressing, and thankfully this recipe can easily be doubled so it's always on hand. Be sure to try it on a simple salad or over any of your favorite grilled vegetables, such as summer squash, bell peppers, and eggplant.

1 small shallot, minced

2 tablespoons honey or agave nectar

3 tablespoons sherry vinegar

2 tablespoons balsamic vinegar

3 tablespoons extra-virgin olive oil

¼ cup canola oil

1 teaspoon coarse salt

½ teaspoon freshly ground black pepper

IN A SMALL MIXING BOWL OR MASON JAR, combine the shallot, honey, sherry and balsamic vinegars, and olive and canola oils; season with salt and pepper. Whisk or shake to blend. Keep any leftover vinaigrette covered in the refrigerator for up to 1 week.

Makes 1 cup

BLACK KALE, SHIITAKE, KUMQUAT VINAIGRETTE

MAKES 6 CUPS

Raw kale can be a tough sell to some people, but is really easy to love if you treat it right. The bitter green tastes best when the vinaigrette has had a chance to soak into the leaves and soften them a bit. Kale's chewy texture and peppery kick absorbs this robust Kumquat Vinaigrette to create a bold vegetable dish with epic flavor.

1½ pounds Tuscan black kale (also known as cavolo nero), (about 2 bunches), center ribs removed, leaves thinly sliced crosswise

6 shiitake mushrooms, wiped of grit, stemmed, and sliced

½ cup Kumquat Vinaigrette (recipe follows)

½ teaspoon coarse salt

¼ teaspoon freshly ground black pepper

IN A MIXING BOWL, combine the kale, mushrooms, vinaigrette, salt, and pepper. Toss thoroughly and allow the ingredients to sit for at least 15 minutes before serving.

KUMQUAT VINAIGRETTE

A mosaic of colors and textures, this Kumquat Vinaigrette has a spicy citrus tang that adds a great pop of flavor and brightness to earthy kale. Wonderfully versatile, you can add a splash to chilled pasta or grains or drizzle on steamed asparagus or your favorite grilled fish.

8 kumquats, halved crosswise, seeded and sliced (about ½ cup)
1 green Thai Bird's Eye chili pepper, minced
2 teaspoons sambal oelek chili paste
2 garlic cloves, minced
¼ cup chopped fresh chives
Juice of 2 to 3 limes (about ¼ cup)
2 tablespoons honey or agave nectar
1 teaspoon coarse salt
¼ cup extra-virgin olive oil
¼ cup canola oil

TO PREPARE THE VINAIGRETTE, in a mixing bowl combine the kumquats, chili, chilipaste, garlic, chives, lime juice, honey, and salt. Gently blend with a whisk. Pour in the olive and canola oils all at once and lightly whisk until the ingredients just come together; this is not an emulsified vinaigrette. Pour the vinaigrette into a plastic container or jar and shake it up just before you are ready to dress the vegetables. Keep any leftover covered in the refrigerator for up to 1 week.

Makes 1½ cups

BLACK KALE

Once you've tried black kale, you might not ever want to go back to the more conventional supermarket variety. Also known as Tuscan, dinosaur, lacinato kale, and cavolo nero, this Italian variety has long, spiky, ruffled deep green leaves with long ribs. It is less bitter than curly kale, and has an earthier, more delicate taste. Kale is one of the most nutritious vegetables on the planet, to boot!

KUMQUATS

Resembling miniature oranges, kumquats are little bursts of sweet and sour. As kids, my sister and I would eat them right off the trees: bite, pucker, and smile. The beauty is that you eat the whole fruit, skin and all. The sweetness is in the skin, while the tart is in the fruit—it's backward from typical citrus. When seeding kumquats, use a toothpick to get them all out.

SAMBAL OELEK CHILI PASTE

Unlike bottled hot sauces, like Tabasco, sambal is a thick, brick red chili paste that adds a deep fiery flavor without being too vinegary or overbearing. A couple of spoonfuls of sambal can enliven eggs, soup, plain rice, or a stir-fry. You will find sambal in a jar at Asian markets or in the international aisle at the grocery store.

CABBAGE, GREEN APPLE, SUNFLOWER SEED, FERMENTED BLACK BEAN VINAIGRETTE

MAKES 4 CUPS

A tantalizing combination of textures and tastes, this vibrant slaw/salad is one of those make-ahead dishes where luckily the flavors develop as it sits. Crunchy and sweet, this cabbage slaw is a fresh, crisp accompaniment to any main protein on the picnic menu! Use the cabbage as a topping for fish tacos or as sandwich slaw for Miso Salmon (page 97) and Seared Ahi Tuna (page 103).

½ head red cabbage
1 large Granny Smith apple, halved lengthwise, cored, and chopped (see page 9)
3 scallions, white and green parts, chopped
3 tablespoons sunflower seeds, toasted and salted
¼ cup whole almonds, toasted and crushed (see page 3)
½ cup coarsely chopped fresh cilantro leaves
½ cup Fermented Black Bean Vinaigrette (recipe follows)
Coarse salt
Freshly ground black pepper

CUT THE CABBAGE IN HALF AND CUT AWAY THE CORE, then thinly slice the cabbage wedges crosswise into shreds. Rinse the cabbage in a colander and allow to drain thoroughly.

IN A LARGE MIXING BOWL, combine the cabbage, apple, scallions, sunflower seeds, almonds, and cilantro. Pour the vinaigrette over the ingredients and toss gently. Season with salt and pepper.

FERMENTED BLACK BEAN VINAIGRETTE

I swear this is one of those recipes that tastes better than it looks! Fermented black beans are like an assertive soy sauce, with complex flavor that lingers in a musky-funky place—in a good way! As a main meal variation, this vinaigrette doubles as a sauce or marinade happy to join tofu and asparagus. Once you try it, trust you'll always have it on the fridge door.

2 tablespoons fermented black
   beans, rinsed
2 anchovies in oil, drained, rinsed,
   and chopped
¼ cup coarsely chopped fresh
   flat-leaf parsley leaves
10 fresh chive sprigs, coarsely
   chopped
2 tablespoons seasoned rice vinegar
Juice of 1 lime
1 tablespoon sesame oil
1 cup canola oil
1 teaspoon freshly ground black
   pepper

IN A BLENDER, combine the fermented black beans, anchovies, parsley, chives, vinegar, lime juice, and sesame oil. Blend until smooth. With the motor running, slowly add the canola oil until emulsified. Season with pepper. Keep any leftover vinaigrette covered in the refrigerator for up to 1 week.

Makes 2 cups

FERMENTED BLACK BEANS

These are not the black beans you find in Mexican cooking but in fact, black soybeans—the same as in miso and soy sauce. Dried and fermented with salt, the process turns the beans soft, savory, umami-tasting, and delicious.

The most common way to feature fermented black beans is in stir-fries, or as a meat rub. I like sneaking the black beans into a vinaigrette for an unexpected, almost odd-tasting surprise to a seemingly middle-of-the-road vegetable dish. Fermented black beans are typically inexpensive and sold in either plastic bags or jars. Check your local Asian market or the international aisle of your supermarket. A little goes a long way, and they keep almost indefinitely!

CITRUS-BRAISED CABBAGE, APPLE, GOAT CHEESE, RED WINE VINEGAR

MAKES 8 CUPS

My grandmother was part German, so it's no surprise that German-Hungarian food plays a large part in my absolute genetic addiction to comfort foods like braised cabbage. Growing up, I'd spend weekends at her house and she would make something like this—without the goat cheese, way too modern for her! Serve the Citrus-Braised Cabbage chilled (without the goat cheese) as a topping for Jackson's Pulled Pork sandwich (page 145) or warm as a side for roasted meats.

1 tablespoon olive oil

1 large red onion, halved lengthwise and sliced

2 Granny Smith apples, halved lengthwise, cored, and sliced (see page 9)

1 head red cabbage (about 2 pounds)

½ cup red wine vinegar

½ cup orange juice

1 tablespoon sugar

1 tablespoon coarse salt, plus more for seasoning

1 teaspoon freshly ground black pepper, plus more for seasoning

4 ounces soft goat cheese, crumbled (¾ cup)

½ cup coarsely chopped fresh flat-leaf parsley

QUARTER THE CABBAGE AND CUT AWAY THE CORE, then thinly slice the wedges crosswise into shreds. Rinse the cabbage in a colander and allow to drain thoroughly.

Coat a large pot with the oil and place over medium heat. When the oil is hot, add the onion and apples. Cook and stir until tender and fragrant, about 3 minutes.

ADD THE CABBAGE TO THE POT, stirring to incorporate. When the cabbage begins to wilt, add the vinegar, orange juice, sugar, 1 tablespoon salt, and 1 teaspoon pepper. Stir everything together to fully incorporate. Cover the pot, reduce the heat to low, and simmer for 20 minutes until the cabbage is soft, stirring from time to time.

PUT THE BRAISED CABBAGE IN A MIXING BOWL and set aside in the fridge to chill. Add the cheese and parsley. Season with salt and pepper before serving.

BLUE LAKE GREEN BEAN,
SHAVED PARMESAN, CAESAR DRESSING

MAKES 4 CUPS

Any green beans will work for this summer dish but I prefer blue lake for their crispness and ability to stand up to robust Caesar dressing. The bean's unique flavor is distinctively mild, subtly grassy, and sweet, with a crisp-tender texture. This green bean dish is best eaten within a couple of hours.

1 pound green beans, preferably blue lake green beans, ends trimmed
½ cup Caesar Dressing (recipe follows)
½ cup shaved Parmesan cheese (about 1 ounce)
Coarse salt and freshly ground black pepper

BRING A LARGE POT OF WELL SALTED WATER TO A BOIL over high heat. Prepare an ice bath by filling a large bowl halfway with water and adding a tray of ice cubes.

BLANCH THE GREEN BEANS for only about 2 minutes; they become tender very quickly. Using a slotted spoon, remove the beans from the water and plunge into the ice bath to "shock" them, i.e., to stop the cooking process and cool them down right away. This procedure also sets the vibrant green color of the beans. Once the beans are completely cool, drain in a colander. The green beans can easily be prepared in advance, covered, and refrigerated.

CUT THE BLANCHED GREEN BEANS into 2-inch pieces and put in a mixing bowl. Add the dressing and cheese. Toss gently to evenly coat. Season with salt and pepper.

CAESAR DRESSING

Creamy, thick, and pungent with garlic, everyone has his or her own recipe for Caesar dressing. This classic version is as simple as it gets, thanks to a blender. Whatever you do, please don't skimp out on the anchovy part. The little fishes give the dressing a salty-briny depth that can't be substituted. The Caesar Club is not to be missed (page 156)!

1 large egg yolk (see page 10)
1 teaspoon Dijon mustard
2 anchovy fillets packed in oil, drained
2 garlic cloves, smashed
1 tablespoon red wine vinegar
Juice of ½ lemon
½ teaspoon Worcestershire sauce
½ teaspoon hot pepper sauce,
   such as Tabasco
¾ cup canola oil
3 tablespoons grated Parmesan cheese,
   preferably Parmigiano-Reggiano

IN A BLENDER, combine the egg yolk, mustard, anchovies, garlic, vinegar, lemon juice, Worcestershire, and hot pepper sauce. Blend on medium speed for a few seconds, and then reduce the speed to low. With the motor running, slowly add the oil until emulsified. Pour into a container or jar and mix in the cheese. Keep any leftover vinaigrette covered in the refrigerator for up to 2 days.

Makes 1 cup

BUTTERNUT SQUASH,
CHIVES, LEMON-TRUFFLE VINAIGRETTE

MAKES 4 CUPS

Consider this recipe a blueprint for serving up any hard winter squash, such as kobucha or acorn. The vegetable's strong, sturdy flavor stands up beautifully to the sensual aroma of truffle oil and the blanket of velvety cream.

1 butternut squash (about 1½ pounds)
   or 5 cups precut butternut squash
   cubes
¼ cup olive oil
Coarse salt
Freshly ground black pepper
1 teaspoon white truffle oil
⅓ cup Lemon-Truffle Vinaigrette
   (recipe follows)
⅓ cup heavy cream
⅓ cup chopped fresh chives

BUTTERNUT SQUASH

Cutting up butternut squash is a notoriously difficult task because of the thickness and shape of the squash. The most important thing to consider when cutting winter squash is to keep it as stable as possible. If you prefer, most supermarkets sell squash already chopped into pieces. This is a great time-saver, since all of the peeling, seeding, and chopping is already done for you.

PREHEAT THE OVEN TO 400 DEGREES F.

USING A SERRATED KNIFE, cut off about ¼ inch from the bottom of the squash, then cut off ¼ inch from the stem end. Lay the squash down on the cutting board and cut crosswise in half through the middle. Stand the squash halves upright on a cutting board, cut-side down (it shouldn't wobble) and cut off the skin with the knife or sharp vegetable peeler, turning the squash as you go. Now, cut the 2 pieces of peeled squash from top to bottom down the middle so you have 4 pieces. Using a tablespoon, scoop out the seeds and strings. Working with 1 piece at a time, cut the squash into ½-inch cubes.

PLACE THE SQUASH ON A LARGE BAKING PAN, drizzle with the olive oil, toss to coat, and spread out in a single layer. Sprinkle with salt and pepper. Roast until the squash has a golden color and is tender when pierced with a fork, about 20 minutes. Transfer the roasted squash to a mixing bowl and set aside to cool. The squash can easily be prepared in advance, covered, and refrigerated.

TO THE COOLED BUTTERNUT SQUASH, add the truffle oil, vinaigrette, cream, and chives. Toss to coat evenly. Season with salt and pepper. May be served warm, cold, or at room temperature.

LEMON-TRUFFLE VINAIGRETTE

Simply omit the truffle oil for an all-purpose Lemon Vinaigrette, used throughout the recipes in book.

Juice of 2 lemons
¾ cup canola oil
2 tablespoons extra-virgin olive oil
¼ teaspoon white truffle oil
1 teaspoon coarse salt
½ teaspoon freshly ground black
   pepper

IN A SMALL MIXING BOWL OR MASON JAR, combine the lemon juice, canola, olive and truffle oils; season with salt and pepper. Whisk or shake to blend. Keep any leftover vinaigrette covered in the refrigerator for up to 1 week.

Makes 1 cup

ORECCHIETTE PASTA, TOMATO, MOZZARELLA, RED PEPPER VINAIGRETTE

MAKES 4 CUPS

Not your standard "macaroni salad," this Italian-style orecchiette pasta shows off its "little ears" in a tangy red pepper vinaigrette. Tossed with sweet baby tomatoes and cubes of creamy mozzarella, this dish is a colorful addition to your summertime menu.

½ pound orecchiette pasta
2 cups cherry or grape tomatoes, halved crosswise
1 cup perlini mozzarella or quartered bocconcini mozzarella balls, water drained
1 cup fresh basil leaves, hand torn
¾ cup Red Pepper Vinaigrette (recipe follows)
Coarse salt
Freshly ground black pepper

BRING A LARGE POT OF WELL-SALTED WATER TO A BOIL OVER HIGH HEAT AND ADD THE PASTA. Give the pasta a stir and cook for 12 minutes or until tender yet firm (al dente). Drain the pasta in a colander and rinse under cool water, allowing the pasta to drain dry. The pasta can easily be prepared in advance, covered, and refrigerated.

PUT THE COOKED, COOLED PASTA IN A MIXING BOWL; add the tomatoes, mozzarella, and basil. Pour in the vinaigrette and toss to coat everything evenly. Season with salt and pepper. May be served warm, cold, or at room temperature.

RED PEPPER VINAIGRETTE

I've always possessed a palate for new and different flavors, with a willingness to put together interesting ingredients that involve unorthodox flavor combinations. Food doesn't have to be strictly Italian, for instance; it can borrow from many cuisines. Here, roasted red pepper vinaigrette comes alive with the addition of typically Asian ingredients like ginger, sesame oil, and mirin. The interplay creates an unexpected flavor combination that comes across with marvelous clarity and dimension.

2 jarred roasted red bell peppers, rinsed, patted dry, and coarsely chopped (about ¾ cup)
½-inch piece fresh ginger, peeled and coarsely chopped (about 1½ teaspoons)
1 garlic clove, smashed
2 tablespoons seasoned rice vinegar
1 teaspoon mirin (Japanese sweet rice wine)
Juice of ½ lime
½ teaspoon coarse salt
½ teaspoon freshly ground black pepper
½ cup canola oil
¼ teaspoon sesame oil

IN A BLENDER, combine the red peppers, ginger, garlic, rice vinegar, mirin, lime juice, salt, and pepper. Blend on medium speed for a few seconds, then reduce the speed to low. With the motor running, slowly add the canola and sesame oils until emulsified. Pour into a container or jar. Keep any leftover vinaigrette covered in the refrigerator for up to 1 week.

Makes 1 cup

CHINESE LONG BEAN,
PLUOT PLUM, PLUM VINAIGRETTE

MAKES 4 CUPS

Inspired by Chinese stir-fried Szechuan green beans with sweet-and-sour plum sauce, this summertime dish combines juicy stone fruit with crunchy green beans in a whole new way. The plum vinaigrette imparts the familiar Asian flavors of ginger, vinegar, and soy, making this satisfying vegetable side a lighter, fresher take on the original.

1½ pounds Chinese long beans
   (about 1 bunch)
1 tablespoon canola oil
4 pluot plums, halved, pitted, and
   thinly sliced
⅓ cup Plum Vinaigrette
   (recipe follows)
4 scallions, white and green parts,
   sliced on bias
½ teaspoon coarse salt
¼ teaspoon freshly ground black
   pepper

BRING A LARGE POT OF WELL-SALTED WATER TO A BOIL over high heat. Prepare an ice bath by filling a large bowl halfway with water and adding a tray of ice cubes.

BLANCH THE LONG BEANS for only about 3 minutes; they become tender very quickly. Using a slotted spoon, remove the beans from the water and plunge into the ice bath to "shock" them, i.e., to stop the cooking process and cool them down right away. This procedure also sets the vibrant green color of the beans. Once the beans are completely cool, drain in a colander. The long beans can easily be prepared in advance, covered, and refrigerated.

CUT THE BLANCHED LONG BEANS on the diagonal into 2-inch pieces.

COAT A LARGE SKILLET WITH THE OIL and place over medium-high heat. When the oil is hot, add the long beans and stir-fry until they start to shrivel and turn bright green, about 5 minutes. Remove the long beans to a mixing bowl and set aside to cool.

TO THE COOLED BEANS, add the plums, vinaigrette, and scallions. Season with salt and pepper. Toss gently to combine. May be served warm, cold, or at room temperature.

PLUM VINAIGRETTE

Neither hoisin or plum sauce is right for me on their own, but when blended together the flavors are harmonious. Monterey Park, Los Angeles's mecca for Chinese food, is just a spoonful away with this vinaigrette that can dress anything from dim sum to seared duck breast.

½ cup hoisin sauce
⅓ cup plum sauce
2 tablespoons soy sauce
2 teaspoons sesame oil
2 teaspoons seasoned rice vinegar
1 teaspoon balsamic vinegar
1 small shallot, chopped
2 garlic cloves, smashed
2 teaspoons peeled and chopped
    fresh ginger
½ teaspoon Dijon mustard
½ teaspoon honey or agave nectar

IN A BLENDER, combine the hoisin, plum sauce, soy, sesame oil, rice and balsamic vinegars, shallot, garlic, ginger, mustard, and honey. Blend on high speed for about 1 minute until smooth. Pour into a plastic container or jar and keep any leftover vinaigrette covered in the refrigerator for up to 1 week.

Makes 1 cup

CHINESE LONG BEANS

Also called snake beans or yard long beans, Chinese long beans come in long curly bundles green beans as skinny as a drinking straw. They are tender like string beans, which may be substituted.

PLUOTS

Part plum, part apricot; this stone fruit hybrid is super sweet with a distinctive dinosaur egg-shaped dappled appearance. Crossing a plum and an apricot results in a deeply flavorful fruit that's like a plum in flavor and texture, but sweeter and less acidic like an apricot. With California supplying most of the market, if pluots are not available, feel free to substitute regular plums.

SOBA NOODLES, KIMCHI VEGETABLES, CREAMY SESAME VINAIGRETTE

MAKES 4 CUPS

What makes Los Angeles such a great food town is its ethnic diversity; food that makes you feel plugged into the rhythms of the city just by eating it. The extensive Asian communities throughout L.A. top over one million. The cuisine brings together a seamless medley of sweetness, acidity, spiciness, and fat, and typifies the bold, balanced flavors that good cooking is all about.

2 (8-ounce) bundles soba (Japanese-style buckwheat) noodles
2 cups Kimchi Vegetables (recipe follows), or store bought, drained
½ cup Creamy Sesame Vinaigrette (recipe follows)
4 scallions, white and green parts, chopped
½ cup salted roasted peanuts, chopped

TO PREPARE THE NOODLES, bring a large pot of water to a boil. Add the noodles; stir gently so that they are all immersed in the water. Bring the water back up to a gentle boil, and then lower the heat so that the water is just simmering. Cook for about 7 to 8 minutes, or following the package directions. Test by eating a strand—it should be cooked through, not al dente, but not mushy either. Drain the noodles in a colander. Immediately run cold water over the noodles, swishing the water around to wash off any trace of starch or gumminess. When you're done the water should run clear.

IN A MIXING BOWL, combine the soba noodles with the kimchi, vinaigrette, scallions, and peanuts. Toss well to coat and evenly distribute the ingredients.

KIMCHI VEGETABLES

Korea Town, or "K-Town" as its fondly nicknamed, is a bustling enclave in East L.A. No Korean meal is complete without kimchi, a piquant condiment of fermented vegetables (most popularly cabbage) seasoned with ginger, garlic, and chili. Fermenting the ingredients over several days gives the dish its characteristic tang, but this streamlined rendition offers relatively instant gratification.

1 head Napa cabbage, quartered, cored, and cut crosswise into ½-inch ribbons
1 small red bell pepper, cored, seeded, and thinly sliced
4 red radishes, thinly sliced
4-inch piece daikon radish, peeled and grated
4 cauliflower florets, finely chopped
2 carrots, shredded
3 tablespoons coarse salt
1½ cups seasoned rice vinegar
1 tablespoon soy sauce
1 tablespoon sugar
2-inch piece fresh ginger, peeled and grated (about 2 tablespoons)
6 garlic cloves, grated
3 tablespoons Sambal Oelek chili paste (see page 31)

TO PREPARE THE KIMCHI, put the cabbage, bell pepper, radishes, daikon, cauliflower, and carrots in a large bowl, sprinkle with the salt, and mix well. Set aside at room temperature for 2 hours, tossing occasionally. Rinse the salt off the vegetables with a couple of changes of water. Drain the vegetables well and put them in a bowl.

IN A LARGE MEASURING CUP, combine the vinegar, sugar, and soy, and stir to dissolve. Stir in the ginger, garlic, and chili paste. Pour the vinegar mixture over the vegetables; stir well to combine. Marinate at room temperature for at least 1 hour, or preferably overnight.

Makes 8 cups

CREAMY SESAME VINAIGRETTE

This Creamy Sesame Vinaigrette tastes like an Asian aioli. It emulsifies quickly, and the creaminess adds richness, but not heaviness to the dish.

1 large egg yolk (see page 10)
2 garlic cloves, smashed
1 teaspoon Dijon mustard
2 tablespoons soy sauce
2 tablespoons seasoned rice vinegar
2 teaspoons sesame oil
1 cup canola oil
2 tablespoons sesame seeds, toasted

IN A BLENDER, combine the egg yolk, garlic, mustard, soy, vinegar, and sesame oil. Blend on medium speed for a few seconds, then reduce the speed to low. With the motor running, slowly add the canola oil until emulsified. Pour into a container or jar and mix in the sesame seeds. Keep any leftover vinaigrette covered in the refrigerator for up to 2 days.

Makes 1 cup

minced

brunoise

cubed

bias

julienne

chiffonade

MARKETPLACE VEGETABLES + LEGUMES + GRAINS

THE DISHES IN THIS SECTION EMBODY THE UNIQUE EXPERIENCE OF EATING AT LEMONADE, and are sure to change the way you think about vegetable-based dishes. There are plenty of meat recipes in this book, but these Marketplace Vegetable dishes provide the backbone to our menu.

Legumes like lentils and edamame, grains like farro, quinoa, and rice, are substantial and balanced in their own right. Generally speaking, beans tend to be unvalued and the fact is, many folks sincerely just don't know what to do with them. We always encourage guests to taste the spectrum of Marketplace Vegetables to open up their palate. To expand people's love of vegetables we treat these ingredients the same way we do meat, where the vegetable takes first place and everything else is built around it. The result is an array of colors and textures; an assortment of dishes to share that appeals to anyone, vegetarian or otherwise.

The following recipes feature a stunning assortment of gorgeous dishes, where presentation is just as important as flavor: *Olive Oil–Braised Lima Bean* (page 57) decorated with lemon and Parmesan; *Forbidden Rice, Heart of Palm, Mushroom* (page 62) speckled with jalapeño vinaigrette; *Farro* (page 58) tossed with roasted spaghetti squash and topped with a vibrant drizzle of pomegranate vinaigrette. These delicious dishes make you think about vegetables differently.

ROMANO BEAN, GREAT NORTHERN BEAN, CORN, DIJON

MAKES 4 CUPS

The So-Cal adaptation of country style succotash, this vegetable dish marries the key ingredients of beans and corn to create a modern rendition. Succotash, popular in the American South, is often cooked to death, swimming in a pool of cream and butter. To lighten it up, I've used raw corn, canned white beans, and roasted Romano beans, tossed with a bit of Dijon and sprightly Champagne Vinaigrette.

½ pound Romano beans, green
   or yellow, ends trimmed
2 tablespoons olive oil
Coarse salt
Freshly ground black pepper
1 (15-ounce) can Great Northern
   beans or white kidney beans,
   drained and rinsed

SALAD
1 ear fresh corn, shucked, kernels cut
   from cob (about 1 cup)
2 tablespoons chopped fresh oregano
   leaves
½ cup Champagne Vinaigrette
   (see page 11)
1 teaspoon Dijon mustard

PREHEAT THE OVEN TO 375 DEGREES F.

PUT THE ROMANO BEANS ON A LARGE BAKING PAN, drizzle with the oil, toss to coat, and spread out in a single layer. Season generously with salt and pepper. Roast for 20 minutes until tender and browned on the edges, shaking the pan from time to time. Cut the beans into thirds.

WHEN READY TO PREPARE THE DISH, in a large mixing bowl, combine the roasted Romano beans, white beans, corn, vinaigrette, and mustard. Toss well to thoroughly combine. Season with salt and pepper if needed.

ROMANO BEANS

Also called Italian flat beans, Romano beans are wide, flat, snap beans, that are meatier than regular green beans.

EDAMAME, SNAP PEA,
SESAME VINAIGRETTE

MAKES 4 CUPS

The definition of a great summer vegetable salad is one that's easy to prepare and can sit out for long periods without spoiling. Look no further, this lean green edamame and snap pea dish adds just the right crunch, while sesame, shallot, and chive add another level of texture by coating the vegetables. The best part about this dish is it's so simple to whip up.

½ pound sugar snap peas (2 cups), ends trimmed

2 cups shelled edamame (green soybeans), frozen, thawed, and cooked

1 large shallot, minced

¼ cup chopped fresh chives

½ cup Sesame Vinaigrette (recipe follows)

1 tablespoon black sesame seeds

½ teaspoon coarse salt

¼ teaspoon freshly ground black pepper

BRING A LARGE POT OF WELL-SALTED WATER to a boil over high heat. Prepare an ice bath by filling a large bowl halfway with water and adding a tray of ice cubes.

BLANCH THE SNAP PEAS FOR ONLY ABOUT 2 MINUTES; they become tender very quickly. Using a slotted spoon, remove the snap peas from the water and plunge into the ice bath to "shock" them, i.e., to stop the cooking process and cool them down right away. This procedure also sets the vibrant green color of the peas. Drain the snap peas in a colander.

PUT THE BLANCHED SNAP PEAS IN A MIXING BOWL. Add the edamame, chives, and vinaigrette, tossing to coat. Sprinkle with the sesame seeds, salt, and pepper, tossing well. Serve chilled.

SESAME VINAIGRETTE

With only a handful of ingredients, this Asian-inspired Sesame Vinaigrette makes a terrific dipping sauce for dumplings or as a glaze for grilled chicken, shrimp, or tofu.

½ cup seasoned rice vinegar

2 tablespoons sesame seeds, toasted

1 garlic clove, minced

1 tablespoon Dijon mustard

1 tablespoon soy sauce

¼ cup canola oil

2 tablespoons sesame oil

¼ teaspoon freshly ground black pepper

IN A SMALL MIXING BOWL OR MASON JAR, combine the vinegar, sesame seeds, garlic, mustard, soy sauce, canola and sesame oils; season with pepper. Whisk or shake to blend. Keep any leftover vinaigrette covered in the refrigerator for up to 1 week.

Makes 1 cup

BELUGA LENTIL, QUINOA, PERSIMMON, VOODOO VINAIGRETTE

MAKES 4 CUPS

Packed with lentils, chickpeas, and quinoa, this hearty dish is a protein powerhouse! It's best chilled, so make ahead and bring a batch to work for lunch during the week. If you're not looking for a vegetarian meal, the forthright flavors make a particularly good accompaniment to grilled meat and seafood.

½ cup black lentils (Beluga), picked over and rinsed
1 small onion, halved
1 carrot, cut into chunks
1 celery stalk, cut into chunks
½ cup quinoa, rinsed
2 cups vegetable broth or water
Coarse salt
½ cup garbanzo beans, drained and rinsed
2 plum (Roma) tomatoes, halved lengthwise, seeded, and chopped
1 ripe Fuyu persimmon or Asian pear, peeled and diced
2 crimini mushrooms, wiped of grit, stemmed, and sliced
½ cup Voodoo Vinaigrette (recipe follows)
½ cup fresh basil leaves, chopped
Freshly ground pepper

TO PREPARE THE LENTILS, in a 3-quart pot, combine the lentils with the onion, carrot, and celery, pour in 1 cup of the broth, and bring to a boil. Reduce the heat to low and simmer until the lentils are just tender, 15 to 20 minutes. Drain the lentils and discard the vegetables. Let the lentils cool.

TO PREPARE THE QUINOA: In a 2-quart pot combine the quinoa, the remaining 1 cup of broth, and a few big pinches of salt until boiling. Cover, reduce the heat to low, and simmer until the water is absorbed and the quinoa fluffs up, about 15 minutes. The quinoa is good to go when you can see the curlicue popping out of each grain. The water should be absorbed; if it's not, drain any excess. Remove the quinoa from heat and fluff with a fork. Set aside in the fridge to chill.

IN A LARGE MIXING BOWL, combine the cooked lentils, quinoa, garbanzo beans, tomatoes, persimmon, and mushrooms. Pour the vinaigrette over the ingredients and toss gently. Add the basil, season with salt and pepper, and lightly toss again.

PERSIMMONS

Persimmons are one of those fall fruits people don't know what to do with. It's important to know there are two kinds of persimmons: the Fuyu, the kind you can eat right away, and the Hachiya (Japanese) that if not completely ripe makes your tongue do funny things. For this recipe I use Fuyu, which you can eat when firm, are crisp and sweet like an apple, and are really easy to work with. Generally, the darker the color, the sweeter the taste.

QUINOA

As versatile as rice but with a delicate, nutty flavor, quinoa is a pantry staple both in my home and at the restaurant. I love the texture of quinoa—a bit crunchy and chewy, still firm after cooking—and its nutty, earthy flavor.

If you desire the quinoa to have a nuttier flavor, you can dry roast it before cooking. To dry roast, place the quinoa in a dry skillet over medium-low heat and stir constantly for 5 minutes.

VOODOO VINAIGRETTE

Inspired by French Masala curry, or Vadouvan, this Voodoo Vinaigrette adds a savory, oniony, light curry-scented flavor to anything quickly and easily with just a couple of tablespoons. Its robust flavor packs a wallop, but is ironically delicate at the same time. This sassy sauce can stand up to either a strong flavored fish like salmon, or enliven a mild fillet of sole.

2 tablespoons brown mustard seeds, toasted
2 tablespoons French curry powder
2 tablespoons ground cumin
1½ teaspoons turmeric
1 cup fresh cilantro, coarsely chopped
½ cup fresh basil leaves, coarsely chopped
Juice of 2 lemons (about ¼ cup)
2 tablespoons mirin (Japanese sweet rice wine)
2 tablespoons seasoned rice vinegar
2 tablespoons honey or agave nectar
1 shallot, coarsely chopped
2 garlic cloves, smashed
1 teaspoon ground nutmeg
½ teaspoon ground cloves
½ teaspoon coarse salt
¼ teaspoon freshly ground black pepper
1 cup canola oil

IN A BLENDER, combine mustard seeds, curry powder, cumin, turmeric, cilantro, basil, lemon juice, mirin, vinegar, honey, shallot, garlic, nutmeg, cloves, salt, and pepper. Blend on medium speed for a few seconds, then reduce the speed to low. With the motor running, slowly add the canola oil until emulsified. Pour into a container or jar. Keep any leftover vinaigrette covered in the refrigerator for up to 1 week.

Makes 2 cups

PUY LENTIL, PIQUILLO PEPPER, OLIVE, RED WINE–OREGANO VINAIGRETTE

MAKES 4 CUPS

Simply saying the word "Mediterranean" conjures a wealth of tasty possibilities. The palette of ingredients is as colorful and rich in variety as the countries that make up the region itself. French lentils, Spanish *piquillo* peppers, and Greek Kalamata olives are all pulled together with a zippy Italian red wine vinaigrette. If you're craving meat, serve this lentil side with Greek-Marinated Chicken (page 90) or Lamb Tagine (page 120). The dish is versatile and can be served warm, room temperature, or chilled.

1½ cups Puy (French green) lentils, picked over and rinsed
1 small onion, cut into chunks
1 carrot, cut into chunks
1 celery stalk, cut into chunks
1 quart vegetable broth or water
1 (8-ounce) jar piquillo peppers (about 7), drained and cut into thin strips
½ cup pitted Kalamata olives, sliced
½ cup fresh flat-leaf parsley, coarsely chopped
¾ cup Red Wine–Oregano Vinaigrette (recipe follows)
½ teaspoon coarse salt
¼ teaspoon freshly ground black pepper

TO PREPARE THE LENTILS: In a 3-quart pot, combine the lentils with the onion, carrot, and celery, pour in the broth, and bring to a boil. Reduce the heat to low and simmer until the lentils are just tender, about 20 minutes. Drain the lentils and discard the vegetables. Let the lentils cool.

IN A LARGE MIXING BOWL, combine the cooked lentils, piquillo peppers, and olives. Pour the vinaigrette over the ingredients and toss gently. Add the parsley, season with salt and pepper, and toss again.

PUY LENTILS

These little French legumes have a unique, nutty flavor that's attributed to the volcanic soil they're grown in, which gives this special variety their fine, mineral-rich taste. Consequently, puy lentils have less starch than other green lentils, so they don't get all mushy when you cook them, and they hold their shape. I always keep a bag of puy lentils in my pantry since they can be prepared relatively quickly and make for the base of a stellar side salad, equally good served warm or at room temperature.

RED WINE–OREGANO VINAIGRETTE

While L.A. doesn't have an Italian borough like North Beach in San Francisco or Little Italy in New York City, the city still claims a couple of red-and-white-checkered tablecloth joints that serve stellar old-school Italian food. In honor of local landmarks like Dan Tana's and Miceli's in Hollywood, this Red Wine-Oregano Vinaigrette is as unadulterated as it gets. Fortified with black olives to boast a bit of heft, this recipe is referenced many times in the book and should be a mainstay in your fridge.

¼ cup red wine vinegar
Juice of ½ lemon
5 pitted Kalamata olives, coarsely
   chopped
2 sprigs fresh oregano, leaves
   striped from the stem and coarsely
   chopped
1 garlic clove, coarsely chopped
½ teaspoon honey or agave nectar
⅔ cup extra-virgin olive oil
½ teaspoon coarse salt
¼ teaspoon freshly ground black
   pepper

IN A BLENDER, combine the vinegar, lemon juice, olives, oregano, garlic, honey, oil, salt, and pepper. Blend on high speed for about 1 minute until smooth and thick. Pour into a plastic container or jar and keep any leftover vinaigrette covered in the refrigerator for up to 1 week.

Makes 1 cup

OLIVE OIL-BRAISED LIMA BEAN, LEMON, PARMESAN

MAKES 4 CUPS

I was reluctant at first to put this dish on the Lemonade menu for fear of lima bean's bad childhood rap. Happily, people responded positively and instantly made this dish one of our signatures. Slowly braising the lima beans in fruity olive oil, lemon, and fried garlic chips infuses intense flavor into an otherwise bland-tasting bean. The crispy garlic chip component is not to be missed and stands solid on its own; use as a garnish for just about anything, as an added crunch in sautéed spinach, or crumbled over a steak.

FRIED GARLIC
10 large garlic cloves (1 bulb),
   thinly sliced with a paring knife
¼ cup canola oil

SALAD
2 (10-ounce) package shelled lima
   beans, frozen and thawed (4 cups)
2 cups olive oil
1 lemon, thinly sliced
2 fresh rosemary sprigs
Juice of 1 lemon
1 cup shaved Parmesan cheese,
   (about 2 ounces)
¼ cup chopped fresh flat-leaf parsley
½ teaspoon coarse salt
½ teaspoon freshly ground black
   pepper

TO PREPARE THE CRISPY FRIED GARLIC CHIPS, place a small skillet over medium-low heat and coat with the canola oil. When the oil is hot, add the sliced garlic cloves and cook for only about 1 minute, until the garlic just begins to lightly brown and crisp. Take care not to burn the garlic; you must keep the slices moving around the pan so they don't burn. If they do, start over because nothing worth eating can come after burnt garlic. With a slotted spoon, transfer the fried garlic to a small plate. The leftover garlic oil is terrific for sautéing sliced potatoes.

PUT THE LIMA BEANS IN A 3-QUART POT OVER MEDIUM-LOW HEAT. Add olive oil, lemon slices, rosemary, and half of the fried garlic. Cover and gently simmer until the beans are tender, about 15 minutes. Set the limas, along with the oil and aromatics, aside to cool. The lima beans can easily be prepared in advance, covered, and refrigerated in the olive oil mixture.

WHEN READY TO PREPARE THE DISH, drain the lima beans, rosemary, lemon slices, and fried garlic chips and put them in a large mixing bowl—you may reserve the fragrant olive oil for cooking or bread dipping. To the cooked limas, add the lemon juice, cheese, and parsley. Season with salt and pepper, and toss to combine. To serve, garnish with the remaining crispy fried garlic chips.

FARRO, SPAGHETTI SQUASH, POMEGRANATE VINAIGRETTE

MAKES 4 CUPS

If you haven't gone down the road of spaghetti squash because you're not quite sure what the hell to do with it, let this be the first recipe you try! The "noodles" are a terrific stand-in for carb-dense pasta, firm yet tender, with a bit of bite. Nutty farro, roasted spaghetti squash, sweet, tart cranberries, grassy parsley—are all brought together with a slightly mouth-puckering vinaigrette. Southern California's coastal region has a unique Mediterranean climate found in only five areas of the world, with mild wet winters and hot dry summers. The combination of Mediterranean ingredients sings with color and flavor. For a hot side-dish alternative, omit the Pomegranate Vinaigrette and replace with a pat of butter.

1 spaghetti squash (about 3 pounds), halved lengthwise and seeds removed
2 tablespoons olive oil
Coarse salt
Freshly ground black pepper
1 cup farro
¼ cup fresh flat-leaf parsley, chopped
¼ cup dried cranberries
½ cup Pomegranate Vinaigrette (recipe follows)
¼ cup crumbled feta

PREHEAT THE OVEN TO 375 DEGREES F.

DRIZZLE THE FLESH OF THE SQUASH WITH OIL and season generously with salt and pepper. Place the squash halves, cut-sides down, on a baking pan and roast until fork-tender, about 45 minutes. Scrape squash with a fork to remove flesh in long strands. Put into a large mixing bowl and set aside to cool.

TO PREPARE THE FARRO, bring a 2-quart pot of salted water to a boil. Add the farro, reduce the heat to medium-low, and cover. Simmer until the farro is tender and the grains have split open, about 20 minutes. Drain and rinse with cool water.

ADD THE COOKED AND COOLED FARRO to the bowl of spaghetti squash. Add the parsley and dried cranberries. Drizzle with the vinaigrette, season with salt and pepper, and toss to combine. Crumble the feta on top before serving.

POMEGRANATE VINAIGRETTE

Tartly sweet pomegranate juice is now widely available in supermarkets, making quick work of this Pomegranate Vinaigrette. Splashing on bitter greens, such as arugula, kale, or baby spinach.

1 cup pomegranate juice
¼ cup honey or agave nectar
½ shallot, minced
2 garlic cloves, minced
2 tablespoons red wine vinegar
Juice of 1 lemon
1 cup extra-virgin olive oil
Coarse salt and freshly ground black
  pepper

POUR THE POMEGRANATE JUICE INTO A SMALL POT and place over medium-low heat. Add the honey and gently simmer until the juice has reduced to ¼ cup and is thick and syrupy, roughly 10 minutes. Set aside to cool.

IN A SMALL MIXING BOWL OR MASON JAR, combine the cooled pomegranate syrup, shallot, garlic, vinegar, lemon juice, and oil; season lightly with salt and pepper. Whisk or shake to blend. Reserve at room temperature until needed. Keep any leftover vinaigrette covered in the refrigerator for up to 1 week.

Makes about 1 cup

ISRAELI COUSCOUS,
WILD MUSHROOM, PARMESAN,
LEMON-TRUFFLE VINAIGRETTE

MAKES 4 CUPS

Israeli couscous, sometimes called "pearl pasta," is a delightfully soft, satisfying, healthy "grain" that's a welcome substitute to the average pasta, potato, and rice dishes. Like all starches, couscous provides a versatile foundation upon which you can build any combination of flavors. Here, I've chosen a medley of earthy mushrooms for depth; grainy, aged Parmesan for height, and an herbaceous finish of fresh parsley. This couscous dish makes a terrific side for roasts or grilled meats, and you can add whatever savory ingredients you like to jazz it up.

¾ pound assorted wild mushrooms, such as crimini, shiitake, and oyster, wiped of grit, stemmed, and sliced

2 tablespoons olive oil

Coarse salt

Freshly ground black pepper

1 cup Israeli couscous

1 cup vegetable broth or water

¼ cup Lemon-Truffle Vinaigrette (see page 39)

½ cup shaved Parmesan cheese

¼ cup coarsely chopped fresh flat-leaf parsley

PREHEAT THE OVEN TO 400 DEGREES F.

PUT THE MUSHROOMS ON A LARGE BAKING PAN, drizzle with the oil, toss to coat and spread out in a single layer. Season generously with salt and pepper. Roast, shaking the pan from time to time, until the mushrooms lose their moisture, shrink, and begin to brown, 15 to 20 minutes. Transfer the mushrooms to a mixing bowl and set aside to cool. The mushrooms can easily be prepared in advance, covered, and refrigerated.

TO PREPARE THE COUSCOUS, place a large dry skillet over medium-low heat. Toast the couscous, stirring frequently, until it smells nutty and is golden-brown, about 5 minutes. Pour in the broth, cover, and simmer until the couscous is just tender, 10 to 12 minutes. Set the couscous aside to cool. The couscous can easily be prepared in advance, covered, and refrigerated.

WHEN READY TO PREPARE THE DISH, in a large mixing bowl, combine the cooked, cooled mushrooms, couscous, vinaigrette, cheese, and parsley. Season with salt and pepper, and toss to combine.

FORBIDDEN RICE, HEART OF PALM, MUSHROOM, JALAPEÑO VINAIGRETTE

MAKES 4 CUPS

Without containing any animal protein, this is one meaty meal! Exotic in concept but simple in execution, this refreshing rice dish is a winner. Serve with Seared Ahi Tuna (page 103) or Braised Pork Belly (page 117).

1½ cups black forbidden rice
1½ cups water
1 (15-ounce) can heart of palm, drained, rinsed, and chopped
8 button mushrooms, wiped of grit, stemmed, and sliced
4 scallions, white and green parts, chopped
½ cup Jalapeño Vinaigrette (recipe follows)
1 teaspoon coarse salt
½ teaspoon freshly ground black pepper

FORBIDDEN RICE

Forbidden rice grains look like sexy black leather. Legend has it that Chinese emperors were once the sole consumer of forbidden rice, hence its name. Its firm texture and vaguely smoky taste hold up well to assertive flavors.

PUT THE FORBIDDEN RICE IN A COLANDER under cold running water and rinse until the water runs clear. Drain well.

COMBINE THE RICE AND WATER in a 2-quart pot over medium heat. Bring to a boil, reduce the heat, and simmer for 30 to 35 minutes, uncovered, until the rice is tender but still firm, stirring occasionally. Remove from the heat and let stand for 5 minutes to allow the grains to absorb any remaining liquid; drain any excess.

PUT THE RICE INTO A BOWL and allow to cool to room temperature. The black rice can easily be prepared in advance, covered, and refrigerated.

TO THE COOLED FORBIDDEN RICE, add the mushrooms, scallions, and vinaigrette. Season with salt and pepper; toss thoroughly to combine. May be served warm, cold, or at room temperature.

JALAPEÑO VINAIGRETTE

Layered with warming spices like ginger and cumin and tamed with a smidge of honey, this well-rounded vinaigrette easily doubles as a marinade for chicken or fish.

2 tablespoons seasoned rice vinegar

Juice of 1 lime

1 jalapeño, stemmed, halved lengthwise, seeded if desired, and coarsely chopped

½ inch fresh ginger, peeled and coarsely chopped (about 1 tablespoon)

2 tablespoons coarsely chopped fresh flat-leaf parsley

1 teaspoon Dijon mustard

1 teaspoon honey or agave nectar

1 teaspoon coarse salt

½ teaspoon freshly ground black pepper

¼ teaspoon ground cumin

¾ cup canola oil

IN A BLENDER, combine the vinegar, lime juice, jalapeño, ginger, parsley, mustard, honey, salt, pepper, and cumin. Blend on medium speed for a few seconds, then reduce the speed to low. With the motor running, slowly add the oil until emulsified. Pour into a container or jar. Keep any leftover vinaigrette covered in the refrigerator for up to 1 week.

Makes 1 cup

RICE PILAF, NECTARINE, WHITE CHEDDAR, MINT VINAIGRETTE

MAKES 4 CUPS

Many foods benefit from toasting to bring out more flavors, such as spices and nuts. The same goes for grains, especially in this preparation. Basmati and orzo are pan-toasted before boiling in the broth to bring out an unmistakable depth of character. Combining the grains with juicy nectarines, mint, and sharp cheddar cheese creates a satisfying dish.

2 tablespoons canola oil
½ cup basmati rice
½ cup orzo
2 cups vegetable broth or water
½ cup Mint Vinaigrette (recipe follows)
2 ripe white nectarines, halved, pitted, and cubed (about 2 cups)
¾ cup shredded sharp white cheddar
¼ cup fresh mint leaves, coarsely chopped
½ teaspoon coarse salt
¼ teaspoon freshly ground black pepper

BASMATI RICE

Literally translated as "queen of fragrance," basmati has been grown in the foothills of the Himalayas for thousands of years. Basmati is a slim, long-grained rice with a fine texture and nutlike flavor and aroma. Its distinctive qualities can be attributed to the fact that the grain is aged to decrease its moisture content. It can be found widely in Indian and Middle Eastern stores and most supermarkets.

TO PREPARE THE RICE: Place a 2-quart pot over medium heat and coat with 1 tablespoon of the oil. When the oil is hot, add the rice, and stir for a minute or two until the grains are well coated and opaque. Take care not to let the rice brown; this will ensure that the rice stays separate and fluffy. Pour in 1 cup of the broth and bring to a boil. Cover tightly and reduce the heat to low. Allow the rice to steam for 20 to 25 minutes or until all of the liquid is absorbed. Set aside to cool. The rice can easily be prepared in advance, covered, and refrigerated.

TO PREPARE THE ORZO: Place a separate small pot over medium heat and coat with the remaining 1 tablespoon of the oil. When the oil is hot, add the orzo and cook, stirring frequently, until the orzo starts to toast and is lightly browned and golden, 5 to 6 minutes. Pour in the remaining 1 cup of the broth and bring to a boil. Simmer, uncovered, until the orzo is just tender, 8 to 10 minutes. Drain well. Set aside to cool. The orzo can easily be prepared in advance, covered, and refrigerated.

WHEN READY TO PREPARE THE DISH, in a large mixing bowl, combine the cooled rice, orzo, vinaigrette, nectarines, cheese, and mint. Season with salt and pepper, and toss to combine.

MINT VINAIGRETTE

The sunny fresh flavors of cool, refreshing mint and mildly acidic Champagne vinegar combine to make a lively dressing that adds *oomph* to salads, roasted vegetables, and grain dishes.

1 cup fresh mint leaves, finely
   chopped
⅓ cup Champagne vinegar
1 tablespoon honey or agave nectar
½ cup canola oil
½ teaspoon coarse salt
¼ teaspoon freshly ground black
   pepper

IN A SMALL MIXING BOWL OR MASON JAR, combine the mint, vinegar, honey, and oil; season with salt and pepper. Whisk or shake to blend. Keep any leftover vinaigrette covered in the refrigerator for up to 1 week.

Makes about 1 cup

MARKETPLACE VEGETABLES + PROTEIN

IT'S NOT JUST L.A., but today we live in a time where people are very sensitive to their diet, garnering a lot of attention to selective eating, where we've all become conscious of what we eat, whether simply for a healthy lifestyle or out of necessity. While the Marketplace Vegetables comprise most of Lemonade's menu, some folks simply need a bit of added protein to make a "complete" meal, so this chapter delivers that.

Leftovers from LAND + SEA (pages 86–105) make their way into these fully realized dishes, whether its *Tandoori Chicken, Mango, Coconut, Tamarind Vinaigrette* (page 80) or *Skirt Steak, Balsamic Bermuda Onion, Poblano Pepper* (page 76). Here, lean leftovers of seared tuna, baked chicken, and grilled steak are not second-string afterthoughts, but instead bump up Marketplace Vegetables to create meals that are equally light and satisfying.

AHI TUNA, SNAP PEA, WATERMELON RADISH, GINGER VINAIGRETTE

MAKES 4 CUPS

Sugar snap peas have the same lively sweetness as shelled peas but are eaten pod and all! If snap peas aren't available, substitute green beans. The colorful combination of ruby tuna, green peas, and magenta radishes is dressed with tangy Ginger Vinaigrette for a light lunch or refreshing side dish.

½ **pound Seared Ahi Tuna (see page 103), cooled and cut into ¼ inch chunks**
½ **pound sugar snap peas, strings removed and cut into thirds**
2 **watermelon radishes or 6 regular radishes, halved and thinly sliced**
1 **teaspoon white sesame seeds, toasted**
1 **teaspoon black sesame seeds**
½ **cup Ginger Vinaigrette (recipe follows)**
¼ **cup fresh mint leaves, coarsely chopped**
½ **teaspoon coarse salt**
¼ **teaspoon freshly ground black pepper**

IN A MIXING BOWL, combine the seared tuna, snap peas, radishes, and sesame seeds. Drizzle with the vinaigrette, add the mint, season with salt and pepper, and toss well to combine. Chill for 30 minutes to 1 hour to allow the flavors to come together.

WATERMELON RADISH

From the outside they don't look like much—just an ordinary turnip or radish with a green hue—but inside bursts a seductive raspberry pink. They're super crunchy, with just a hint of peppery bite, and surprisingly sweeter than you might expect from a normal radish. A mandolin is ideal for slicing these beauties into perfectly thin half moons, but a sharp knife will do. If watermelon radishes are not available, daikon or regular radishes make fine substitutes.

GINGER VINAIGRETTE

Try tossing this Ginger Vinaigrette with rice noodles, or use as a dipping sauce for pot stickers or spring rolls.

2 tablespoons soy sauce

1 tablespoon red wine vinegar

1 teaspoon sesame oil

2 teaspoons peeled and grated fresh ginger

2 teaspoons honey or agave nectar

1 garlic clove, smashed

1 teaspoon Dijon mustard

1 teaspoon sesame seeds, toasted

1 cup canola oil

¼ teaspoon freshly ground black pepper

IN A BLENDER, combine the soy, vinegar, sesame oil, ginger, honey, garlic, mustard, and sesame seeds. Blend until smooth. With the motor running, slowly add the canola oil until emulsified. Season with pepper. Keep any leftover vinaigrette covered in the refrigerator for up to 1 week.

Makes about 1 cup

BAY SHRIMP, CANNELLINI BEAN, SHALLOT, CAYENNE

MAKES 4 CUPS

This rustic dish combines some of my favorite Tuscan ingredients—beans, seafood, garlic, lemon, herbs, and fruity olive oil. Fresh herbs make all the difference, adding a powerful pop of flavor to the tender shrimp and white beans. To save on time, use good-quality frozen shrimp and canned cannellini beans. This light, summery dish is effortless on evenings when you're looking for a light meal that can be made quickly, and even ahead of time. Don't dare toss the leftover garlic-lemon oil; serve with grilled baguette.

FRIED GARLIC
10 large garlic cloves (about 1 bulb),
    thinly sliced on a mandolin or with
    a paring knife
¼ cup canola oil

SALAD
1 (15-ounce) can cannellini (white)
    beans, drained and rinsed
2 cups olive oil
1 lemon, cut into thin slices
2 fresh rosemary sprigs
1 pound cooked Bay or Rock shrimp,
    frozen and thawed
¼ cup chopped fresh flat-leaf parsley
¼ cup chopped fresh chives
1 large shallot, chopped
½ cup Champagne Vinaigrette
    (see page 11)
2 teaspoons cayenne pepper
½ teaspoon coarse salt
¼ teaspoon freshly ground black
    pepper

TO PREPARE THE CRISPY FRIED GARLIC CHIPS, place a small skillet over medium-low heat and coat with the canola oil. When the oil is hot, add the sliced garlic cloves and cook for only 2 to 3 minutes, until the garlic just begins to lightly brown and crisp. Take care not to burn the garlic; you must keep the slices moving around the pan so they don't burn. If they do, start over because nothing worth eating can come after burnt garlic. With a slotted spoon, transfer the fried garlic to a small plate. The leftover garlic oil is terrific for sautéing sliced potatoes.

PUT THE CANNELLINI BEANS in a 3-quart pot over medium-low heat, cover with the olive oil, lemon, rosemary, and half of the fried garlic. Cover and gently simmer until the beans are tender, about 15 minutes. Set the beans, along with the oil and aromatics, aside to cool. The cannellini beans can easily be prepared in advance, covered, and refrigerated in the olive oil mixture.

WHEN READY TO PREPARE THE DISH, drain the cannellini beans, rosemary, preserved lemon, and fried garlic chips and put them in a large mixing bowl—you may reserve the fragrant olive oil for cooking or bread dipping. To the cooked beans, add the shrimp, parsley, chives, shallot, vinaigrette, and cayenne. Season with salt and pepper, and toss to combine. Chill for 30 minutes to 1 hour to allow the flavors to come together. To serve, garnish with the remaining crispy fried garlic chips.

SMOKED SALMON, WATERCRESS, CUCUMBER, BAGEL CROUTONS, HORSERADISH DRESSING

MAKES 4 CUPS

Growing up in L.A., I'm confident to say that Nate 'n Al's is the best Jewish deli on the West Coast. It's been around forever. Located within easy walking distance of glittery Rodeo Drive in Beverly Hills, this old-world-style delicatessen is anything but posh. Sunday breakfasts are the best; I order a bagel with the works: a schmear of cream cheese, slices of red onion, juicy tomato, crunchy cucumber, a smattering of salty capers . . . crowned with a thin veil of salmon lox. Here, all of those ingredients find themselves reinvigorated when transformed into a salad. I prefer using cryovacted blocks of smoked salmon as opposed to traditional sliced lox. The taste and flaky texture of a chunked smoked salmon takes the familiar flavor combination to new heights.

1 sesame or onion bagel, cut into
  ½-inch cubes
2 tablespoons canola oil plus ¼ cup
Coarse salt and freshly ground black
  pepper
½ cup capers, drained and dried well,
  or caperberries, sliced
1 bunch watercress or arugula (about
  2 cups), tough stems removed
½ hothouse cucumber, ends trimmed,
  halved lengthwise, seeds scooped
  out with a spoon, halved again,
  and sliced
½ cup cherry or grape tomatoes,
  halved crosswise
½ cup Pickled Red Onion
  (see page 4), chopped
2 (4-ounce) blocks smoked salmon,
  cut into small chunks
½ cup Horseradish Dressing
  (recipe follows)

TO PREPARE THE BAGEL CROUTONS, PREHEAT THE OVEN TO 350 DEGREES F.

PUT THE BAGEL CUBES ON A LARGE BAKING PAN, drizzle with 2 tablespoons of the oil, toss to coat, and spread out in a single layer. Season generously with salt and pepper. Bake, shaking the pan from time to time, until the croutons are firm and lightly golden, 10 to 15 minutes. You should have about 1 cup of croutons. The croutons can easily be prepared in advance, covered, and kept at room temperature.

TO PREPARE THE CRISPY CAPERS, pour the remaining ¼ cup of oil into a small skillet or pot and place over medium heat. Carefully add the capers to the hot oil (they will spit and bubble). Shake the pan or gently stir until the capers are puffed and crisp, 1 minute. Remove the capers with a slotted spoon to a plate lined with paper towels. The crispy capers can easily be prepared in advance, covered, and kept at room temperature.

TO PREPARE THE SALAD, combine the watercress, cucumber, tomatoes, pickled onion, and salmon. Drizzle with the dressing, tossing well to coat the ingredients. Add the bagel croutons and crispy capers, tossing again to evenly distribute. Serve chilled or at room temperature.

HORSERADISH DRESSING

Horseradish turns up the heat in this tangy cold dressing with a kick. Spread it on your favorite sandwich, or drizzle over Grilled Skirt Steak (page 104) or baked salmon.

½ cup crème fraîche, sour cream, or plain nonfat Greek yogurt

2 tablespoons cream cheese, at room temperature

¼ cup grated fresh or prepared horseradish

2 tablespoons coarsely chopped fresh dill

Juice of ½ lemon

1 tablespoon white or apple cider vinegar

½ teaspoon coarse salt

¼ teaspoon freshly ground black pepper

IN A MIXING BOWL, combine the crème fraîche, cream cheese, horseradish, dill, lemon, vinegar, salt, and pepper. Mix well with a small whisk until the dressing is well combined and smooth. Stir in 1 tablespoon of water or lemon juice to thin out if needed. Cover and refrigerate until ready to use. Keep any leftover vinaigrette covered in the refrigerator for up to 1 week.

Makes 1 cup

SKIRT STEAK, BALSAMIC BERMUDA ONION, POBLANO PEPPER

MAKES 4 CUPS

Skirt steak is an incredibly tasty cut; when paired with tender radicchio and smoky poblano pepper, it becomes a hearty main-course meal. This is one of my favorite recipes to prepare for an afternoon cookout. Often I crave to sink my teeth into a piece of meat but don't want filling potatoes with it. This steak dish is light and satisfying and so easy to throw together. I'm a believer that opposites do attract. Hot and cold plays off of each other, with the grilled meaty steak and the cool crispness of the greens.

BALSAMIC ONIONS
1 red onion, cut into ¼-inch-thick
   slices
¼ cup balsamic vinegar
¼ cup sherry vinegar
¼ cup canola oil
2 garlic cloves, grated

SALAD
1 poblano pepper
1 small head radicchio (about
   6 ounces)
2 cups mizuna or baby mixed greens
½ pound Grilled Skirt Steak (see page
   104), sliced
½ cup crumbled feta
¼ cup Red Wine–Oregano Vinaigrette
   (see page 55)
½ teaspoon coarse salt
¼ teaspoon freshly ground black
   pepper

TO PREPARE THE ONIONS, put them in a small bowl, and add the balsamic and sherry vinegars, oil, and garlic. Set aside at room temperature and allow to marinate for 15 minutes.

PREHEAT AN OUTDOOR GRILL OR GRILL PAN TO MEDIUM-HIGH HEAT. Rub the grill with oil to prevent sticking. Place the pepper on the grill and cook until the skin is charred and blackened on all sides, turning with tongs, about 10 minutes. When cool enough to handle, pull off the skin and stem. It's ok if you don't remove all of the blistered bits, it adds a delicious smoky flavor. Split the pepper, scrape out the core and seeds. Cut into ¼-inch strips and set aside.

DRAIN THE ONIONS FROM THE VINEGAR MIXTURE. Lay the onion slices on the hot grill for 2 minutes, turning often, until charred on both sides. Remove the onion slices from the grill and coarsely chop.

DISCARD ANY LIMP OR LOOSE OUTER LEAVES FROM THE RADICCHIO. Quarter the radicchio through the stem end. Cut the core out, and cut the leaves crosswise into 1-inch pieces. Put the radicchio in a large mixing bowl, add the greens, grilled pepper and onion, steak, feta, and vinaigrette. Season with salt and pepper. Toss the ingredients to combine.

CHINESE-STYLE BRAISED DUCK, RAINBOW CHARD, PINEAPPLE, CASHEW, CHILI-CORIANDER VINAIGRETTE

MAKES 4 CUPS

Rich, meaty duck breast is one of those proteins that marry perfectly with crisp, slightly bitter, Swiss chard and the sweet, acidic pop of pineapple. Topped off with a few toasted cashews for texture, the moist, slightly fatty duck is tossed with bold Chili-Coriander Vinaigrette to cut through the meat's richness. With minimal effort, you can put together a dish brimming with crunch, color, and a bit of Asian spice. Serve as a sophisticated and elegant starter or prepare as part of a multicourse extravaganza.

1 recipe Chinese-Style Braised Duck legs (see page 132), chilled, skin and bones removed, meat shredded

1 bunch rainbow Swiss chard (about ¾ pound)

1 cup diced pineapple, fresh or canned in juice and drained

½ cup cashews, toasted and coarsely chopped (see page 3)

½ cup Chili-Coriander Vinaigrette (recipe follows)

¼ cup fresh cilantro leaves, coarsely chopped

SHRED THE DUCK MEAT USING A FORK or your fingers and put into a mixing bowl.

CUT OUT THE RIBS OF THE SWISS CHARD AND DISCARD. Roll the leaves into a bundle and slice crosswise into 1-inch pieces. Put the chopped chard in a colander and rinse well. Set aside to drain.

TO THE DUCK, ADD THE CHARD, PINEAPPLE, AND CASHEWS. Drizzle with the vinaigrette, season with salt and pepper, add the cilantro, and toss to combine. May be served chilled or at room temperature.

CHILI-CORIANDER VINAIGRETTE

This zesty hot-and-sour Chili-Coriander Vinaigrette is extremely versatile. Try it as a dressing on Asian greens, such as bok choy, or as a dipping sauce for poached shrimp.

¾ cup fresh cilantro leaves, coarsely chopped

2 tablespoons mirin (Japanese sweet rice wine)

2 tablespoons seasoned rice vinegar

1 tablespoon Sambal Oelek chili paste (see page 31)

2 garlic cloves, smashed

2 teaspoons fresh ginger peeled and chopped

2 scallions, white and green parts, coarsely chopped

1 teaspoon coriander seeds

½ cup canola oil

½ teaspoon coarse salt

¼ teaspoon freshly ground black pepper

IN A BLENDER, combine the cilantro, mirin, vinegar, chili paste, garlic, ginger, scallions, coriander, oil, salt, and pepper. Blend on high speed for about 1 minute until smooth and green, scraping down the sides of the blender as needed. Pour into a plastic container or jar. Keep any leftover vinaigrette covered in the refrigerator for up to 5 days.

Makes 1 cup

TANDOORI CHICKEN, MANGO, COCONUT, TAMARIND VINAIGRETTE

MAKES 4 CUPS

Leftover Tandoori Chicken (page 96) makes a wonderful base for this tasty tropical dish. Fresh and light, the intense Indian flavors of the chicken balance with the cubes of sweet mango, the tartness of tamarind, and the confetti of toasted coconut.

¾ **pound Tandoori Chicken (see page 96), cooled and cut into small cubes (about 2 cups)**

2 firm-ripe mangos, peeled, pitted, and cubed

½ **cup shredded sweetened coconut, toasted**

½ **cup Tamarind Vinaigrette (recipe follows)**

½ **cup fresh Thai basil leaves, hand torn**

½ **teaspoon coarse salt**

¼ **teaspoon freshly ground black pepper**

IN A LARGE MIXING BOWL, combine the chicken, mango, and coconut. Pour the vinaigrette over the ingredients and toss gently. Add the basil, season with salt and pepper, and lightly toss again. Serve chilled.

MANGO

The best way to go about cutting a mango is to start with a ripe, but still firm, fruit. Once you learn how to work around the flat seed in the center, the rest is easy. Stand the mango up on a cutting board with the stem end on the bottom. Cut down the side without hitting the seeds. Repeat this cut on the other side. Score the fruit of the mango with a knife in ½-inch segments so that you have created a grid. Cut through the flesh but not through the skin. Press the scored mango half inside out and slice the cubes off very close to the skin.

TAMARIND VINAIGRETTE

A sweet-and-sour delight made with tamarind, lime, and honey, this vinaigrette bursts with flavor. Tamarind is a fruit pulp that is used widely through Africa, India, Asia, and Mexico and is available at specialty food stores and ethnic markets.

**2 tablespoons tamarind paste
   or concentrate**
¼ cup warm water
Juice of 1 lime (about ¼ cup)
1 tablespoon honey or agave nectar
⅓ cup extra-virgin olive oil
½ teaspoon coarse salt
**¼ teaspoon freshly ground black
   pepper**
¼ cup plain nonfat Greek yogurt

IN A SMALL MIXING BOWL OR MASON JAR, combine the tamarind, water, lime juice, honey, and oil; season with salt and pepper. Whisk or shake to blend. Add the yogurt, and whisk again to blend. Keep any leftover vinaigrette covered in the refrigerator for up to 1 week.

Makes 1 cup

HARISSA CHICKEN, BULGUR WHEAT, DAIKON RADISH, APRICOT, PARSLEY VINAIGRETTE

MAKES 4 CUPS

Zankou Chicken is a small family-owned chain of Middle Eastern–inspired foods. Their roasted chicken, pickled radish, tabbouleh, and famed garlic sauce has embraced a beloved following across the Southland. I've taken elements from Zankou's menu to invent the ultimate Lemonade version.

½ cup bulgur wheat, fine to medium grain

½ cup boiling water

1 pound Harissa Chicken Breast (page 89), cooled and cut into cubes

½ cup dried apricots, thinly sliced

2-inch piece daikon radish, thinly sliced on a mandolin or with a paring knife

¼ cup fresh mint leaves, hand torn

½ cup Parsley Vinaigrette (recipe follows)

TO PREPARE THE BULGUR, put the bulgur in a bowl and pour in the boiling water to cover. Cover the bowl with a kitchen towel and let it sit for 15 to 20 minutes. All of the water should be absorbed, but if not, drain the excess; fluff the bulgur with a fork. Chill before combining with other ingredients.

TO PREPARE THE SALAD, in a mixing bowl combine the chilled bulgur with the chicken, apricot, radish, and mint. Drizzle with the vinaigrette, season with salt and pepper, and toss to combine. Chill for 30 minutes to 1 hour to allow the flavors to come together.

PARSLEY VINAIGRETTE

Prepare this herbaceous parsley-based vinaigrette as a rustic topping for Grilled Skirt Steak (page 104) or toss with just about any roasted vegetable in season.

1 cup fresh flat-leaf parsley, finely chopped

4 sprigs fresh oregano, leaves striped from the stem and finely chopped

¼ cup red wine vinegar

4 garlic cloves, coarsely chopped

1 jalapeño, minced and seeded if desired

1 cup extra-virgin olive oil

½ teaspoon coarse salt

¼ teaspoon freshly ground black pepper

COMBINE THE PARSLEY, oregano, vinegar, garlic, and jalapeño in a bowl. Whisk in the oil and season with salt and pepper. Mix well and set aside at room temperature to allow the flavors to marry. Keep any leftover vinaigrette covered in the refrigerator for up to 1 week.

Makes about 1½ cups

CHICKEN, JICAMA, TARRAGON,
GREEN GODDESS DRESSING

MAKES 4 CUPS

Laced with the distinctive licorice flavor of tarragon and bathed in zesty Green Goddess Dressing, this easygoing dish will transport you to a back porch in the country.

8 cooked leftover chicken thighs (2 pounds), skin and bones removed, meat cut into thin strips
½ jicama (about 1 pound), peeled, halved, and cut into thin strips
¾ cup Green Goddess Dressing (recipe follows)
½ teaspoon coarse salt
¼ teaspoon freshly ground black pepper
2 fresh tarragon sprigs, leaves striped from the stem and chopped

IN A MIXING BOWL, combine the chicken thigh meat and jicama. Drizzle with the dressing, season with salt and pepper, add the tarragon, and toss to combine.

JICAMA

The crisp, white flesh of this tuber is crunchy, mild, and faintly sweet. To cut, using a serrated knife, slice the jicama in half. Lay each half flat on the cutting board so it's stable and remove the brown skin with a vegetable peeler or knife. Slice the halves into ½-inch-thick slices; lay the slices flat and then cut into ½-inch-thick sticks.

GREEN GODDESS DRESSING

Green goddess dressing has evolved into an American classic. Parsley, tarragon, and chive give this dressing its distinctive green hue. Anchovy and garlic add depth.

½ cup sour cream
¼ cup mayonnaise
1 cup coarsely chopped fresh flat-leaf parsley
2 tablespoons chopped fresh tarragon
2 tablespoons chopped fresh chives
2 tablespoons capers, drained and rinsed
2 anchovy fillets packed in oil, drained
2 garlic cloves, coarsely chopped
Juice ½ lemon
1 tablespoon tarragon or apple cider vinegar
½ teaspoon coarse salt
¼ teaspoon freshly ground black pepper

IN A BLENDER, combine the sour cream, mayonnaise, parsley, tarragon, chives, capers, anchovies, garlic, lemon juice, and vinegar; season with salt and pepper. Blend on high speed for about 1 minute until smooth. Pour the vinaigrette into a plastic container or jar and keep any leftover covered in the refrigerator for up to 1 week.

Makes 1 cup

GREEK-MARINATED CHICKEN, BUTTERNUT SQUASH, GRAPE, RED WINE–OREGANO VINAIGRETTE

MAKES 4 CUPS

Juicy red grapes and crunchy almonds add sweetness and bite to this substantial chicken dish. A collection of textures, shapes, and flavors, this harmonious combination of common ingredients satiates, bite after bite. The yogurt in the Greek-Marinated Chicken (page 90) enhances moisture, so there's no need for added mayonnaise to keep the ingredients peppy. The beauty is it's also travel friendly without the concern of spoilage.

1 butternut squash (about 1½ pounds) or 5 cups precut butternut squash cubes (see page 38)
2 tablespoons olive oil
Coarse salt and freshly ground black pepper
¾ pound Greek-Marinated Chicken (page 90), cooled and cut into ¼-inch cubes (about 3 cups)
1 cup red grapes, halved crosswise
¼ cup fresh flat-leaf parsley leaves
¼ cup slivered almonds, toasted
½ cup Red Wine–Oregano Vinaigrette (page 55)

PREHEAT THE OVEN TO 400 DEGREES F.

USING A SERRATED KNIFE, cut off about ¼ inch from the bottom of the squash, then cut off ¼ inch from the stem end. Lay the squash down on the cutting board and cut crosswise in half through the middle. Stand the squash halves upright on a cutting board, cut-side down (it shouldn't wobble) and cut off the skin with the knife or sharp vegetable peeler, turning the squash as you go. Cut the 2 pieces of peeled squash from top to bottom down the middle so you have 4 pieces. Using a tablespoon, scoop out the seeds and strings. Working with 1 piece at a time, cut the squash into ½-inch cubes.

PUT THE SQUASH ON A LARGE BAKING PAN, drizzle with the olive oil, toss to coat, and spread out in a single layer. Sprinkle generously with salt and pepper. Roast until the squash has a golden color and is tender when pierced with a fork, about 15 minutes, shaking the pan from time to time to brown the squash evenly.

TRANSFER THE ROASTED SQUASH to a mixing bowl and set aside to cool. The squash can easily be prepared in advance, covered, and refrigerated.

TO THE COOLED BUTTERNUT SQUASH, add the chicken, grapes, parsley, almonds, and vinaigrette. Season with salt and pepper, tossing to combine. Serve chilled.

LAND + SEA

LEMONADE IS ALL ABOUT CHOICE. Typically if you go to a fine-dining restaurant, the protein is in the center of the plate and the vegetables are secondary around it. In Southern California, we think the opposite and flip the components around. The colorful varieties of MARKETPLACE VEGETABLES (page 1–45) are the backbone to our food and adding protein is à la carte. This allows for total food freedom to mix and match with any of the vegetable dishes you want. Here you can say I like tuna or salmon, but I want it with "xyz."

The fish, steak, and poultry recipes that follow stand boldly on their own, playfully inspired by a love of diverse flavors from around the world such as Indian tandoori chicken and Japanese miso salmon, to keep it interesting. Leftovers also spin into a delicious assortment of marketplace vegetables like *Harissa Chicken, Bulgur Wheat, Apricot, Parsley Vinaigrette* (page 82) and sandwiches, *Char Siu Chicken, Black Kale, Kimchi Vegetables* (page 153).

HARISSA CHICKEN BREAST

SERVES 4 — MAKES I CUP SAUCE

Harissa sauce is like the Tunisian version of ketchup, but the condiment maintains a bit more fire. The tongue-tingling flavor is a natural marinade for lean chicken, which soaks up all of the robust spice. The provocative North African chili sauce enhances soups, spikes mayonnaise for sandwiches, and tops eggs.

HARISSA SAUCE

4 guajillo chilies, stemmed and seeded
1 teaspoon cumin seeds
1 teaspoon caraway seeds
1 teaspoon coriander seeds
2 garlic cloves, smashed
Juice of 2 lemons
½ cup canola oil
1 teaspoon coarse salt, plus more for seasoning
4 (6-ounce) skinless boneless chicken breast halves
¼ teaspoon freshly ground black pepper

GUAJILLO CHILI

One of the most widely used dried chiles from Mexico, the guajillo is mild to medium hot, and has dark, reddish brown, leathery skin. It has a subtle fruity flavor, with hint of berry.

TO PREPARE THE HARISSA SAUCE, put the chiles in large bowl. Pour enough boiling water over to cover. Drape a kitchen towel over the top to keep the steam in. Let the chiles soak until they're very soft, about 1 hour.

Meanwhile, place a small, dry skillet over low heat and add the cumin, caraway, and coriander seeds. Toast for 1 to 2 minutes until fragrant and lightly toasted, shaking the pan often so the spices don't scorch. In a spice mill, clean coffee grinder, or mortar and pestle, grind the toasted spices into a powder.

DRAIN THE CHILES AND DISCARD THE SOAKING WATER. Transfer the softened chiles to a food processor, add the garlic, lemon juice, and oil; process until the mixture becomes a chunky paste. Transfer the chile paste to a fine-mesh strainer set over a bowl. Press the paste through the strainer into the bowl, discarding the solids. Mix in the toasted ground spices and salt.

PUT THE CHICKEN IN A PLASTIC STORAGE BAG; add the harissa sauce, and smoosh the chicken around to thoroughly coat in the sauce. Press out the air, seal the bag, and marinate the chicken in the refrigerator for at least 24 hours, preferably up to 2 days.

WHEN READY TO COOK THE CHICKEN, preheat the oven to 350 degrees F.

REMOVE THE CHICKEN FROM THE HARISSA, scrape off the excess sauce, and discard. The chicken should have taken on a reddish hue. Put the chicken breasts side-by-side in a baking dish and season both sides generously with salt and pepper. Bake for 30 to 40 minutes until the chicken is cooked through.

GREEK-MARINATED CHICKEN, TZATSIKI

SERVES 4—MAKES 2 CUPS SAUCE

For true tenderizing, the most effective marinades are those that contain dairy products, such as buttermilk and yogurt. Yogurt is mildly acidic, so it doesn't make the meat tough or mushy, the way strongly acidic marinades can. Thick Greek yogurt really sticks to the chicken (and also lamb) and makes the meat tasty and tender. Tzatsiki is a cool cucumber-yogurt sauce that makes a healthful dip for cut-up vegetables. For best results, the chicken needs to marinate for a couple of days, so plan accordingly. Leftovers make a terrific sandwich (page 159).

1 cup plain nonfat Greek yogurt
½ cup fresh oregano leaves, coarsely chopped
1 onion, grated
4 garlic cloves, minced
Juice and finely grated zest of 1 lemon
½ teaspoon red pepper flakes
4 (6-ounce) skinless boneless chicken breast halves
1 tablespoon canola oil
Coarse salt and freshly ground black pepper

TZATSIKI

1 hothouse cucumber, ends trimmed, halved lengthwise, and seeds scooped out with a spoon
2 teaspoons coarse salt
2 cups plain nonfat Greek yogurt
Juice of 2 lemons
1 tablespoon finely chopped fresh dill leaves
2 garlic cloves, minced
½ teaspoon freshly ground black pepper

TO PREPARE THE MARINADE, in a mixing bowl combine the yogurt, oregano, onion, garlic, lemon juice and zest, and red pepper flakes, stirring with a spoon. Put the chicken in a plastic storage bag; add the yogurt mixture, and smoosh the chicken around to thoroughly coat in the marinade. Press out the air, seal the bag, and marinate the chicken in the refrigerator for at least 24 hours, preferably up to 2 days.

TO PREPARE THE TZATSIKI, dice the cucumber into small pieces or shred with the large holes of a box grater. Mix the cucumber pieces in a strainer with the salt, and let stand in the sink or over a bowl for about 30 minutes, shaking and turning a few times to drain the water. After the cucumbers are drained, squeeze them in a dish towel to get out most of the liquid, and transfer them to a large bowl. Using a wooden spoon, stir in the yogurt, lemon juice, dill, garlic, and pepper to combine. Refrigerate the tzatsiki for at least 1 hour to allow the flavors to come together.

WHEN READY TO COOK THE CHICKEN, preheat an outdoor grill or grill pan to medium-high heat. Rub the grates with oil to prevent sticking. Remove the chicken from the marinade, wiping off any excess yogurt so it doesn't burn on the grill. Season both sides of the chicken breasts with a fair amount of salt and pepper. Sear for 8 to 10 minutes, rotating them halfway through cooking to "mark" them. Turn the chicken over and grill the other side for 4 to 6 more minutes. Serve the grilled chicken with the tzatsiki sauce.

BUTTERMILK-BAKED CHICKEN

SERVES 4

The key to any good fried chicken recipe is a buttermilk marinade, and this lightened up version takes the same cue. Thankfully, it's still pretty easy to capture the crunchy goodness of fried chicken with a baked alternative. Buttermilk is slightly acidic, helping to tenderize the chicken and lending a pleasantly tangy flavor. Crispy and moist, the golden brown chicken is excellent right after it comes out of the oven, but its also equally good cold. For a potluck, slice the buttermilk chicken and top with any of the Marketplace Vegetables of your choice, or nestle into a sandwich (page 160). For best results, marinate the chicken for a couple of days, so plan accordingly.

2 cups buttermilk
1 tablespoon Dijon mustard
1 tablespoon hot sauce, such as
   Tabasco
2 teaspoons paprika
1 teaspoon coarse salt, plus more
   for seasoning
1 onion, coarsely chopped
5 garlic cloves, smashed
4 (6-ounce) skinless boneless chicken
   breast halves
2 cups panko (Japanese-style) bread
   crumbs
Freshly ground black pepper
2 tablespoons canola oil

TO PREPARE THE MARINADE, in a large mixing bowl whisk the buttermilk, mustard, hot sauce, paprika, salt, onion, and garlic together to combine. Put the chicken in a plastic storage bag, add the buttermilk mixture, and smoosh the chicken around to thoroughly coat in the marinade. Press out the air, seal the bag, and marinate the chicken in the refrigerator for at least 24 hours, preferably up to 2 days.

WHEN READY TO COOK THE CHICKEN, PREHEAT THE OVEN TO 400 DEGREES F.

REMOVE THE CHICKEN FROM THE MARINADE, wiping off any excess buttermilk, and discard. Season both sides of the chicken breasts lightly with salt and pepper. Spread the breadcrumbs out on a flat plate. Press the chicken breasts into the bread crumbs to completely coat all sides, shaking off the excess.

PUT A CAST-IRON OR OVENPROOF SKILLET OVER MEDIUM-HIGH HEAT. Coat the pan with 2 tablespoons of oil. Once the oil is shimmering, lay the chicken in the pan—you may have to do this in batches. Sear for 3 minutes on each side. Nestle the seared chicken breasts side by side in the skillet. Transfer the skillet (and chicken) to the oven and bake for roughly 20 to 25 minutes, or until the chicken is cooked through and the crust is golden.

CHAR SIU CHICKEN

SERVES 4

Take a stroll through any Chinatown in the world and you're bound to see restaurants with strips of mahogany-colored barbecued pork hanging from hooks in the windows. Char Siu is vital to Chinese barbecue, moist and flavorful on the inside, caramelized and sticky on the outside. The sweet and tangy marinade enlivens chicken equally as well as it does traditional pork. Leftover char siu spawns into a multicultural sandwich with the help of kale and kimchi (page 153). For best results, the chicken needs to marinate for 24 hours, so plan accordingly.

¼ cup soy sauce

¼ cup hoisin sauce

3 tablespoons honey

1-inch piece of fresh ginger, peeled and grated (about 1 tablespoon)

2 tablespoons tamarind paste or concentrate

2 tablespoons white vinegar

3 garlic cloves, coarsely chopped

1 teaspoon Chinese five-spice powder

6 skinless boneless chicken thighs (about 2 pounds)

1 tablespoon canola oil

Coarse salt

Freshly ground black pepper

TO PREPARE THE MARINADE, in a mixing bowl, combine the soy, hoisin, honey, ginger, tamarind, vinegar, and garlic (you should have about 1 cup). Put the chicken in a plastic storage bag, add the marinade, and smoosh the chicken around to thoroughly coat. Press out the air, seal the bag, and marinate the chicken in the refrigerator for at least 2 hours or preferably, overnight.

WHEN READY TO COOK THE CHICKEN, preheat an outdoor grill or grill pan to medium-high heat. Rub the grill with oil to prevent sticking. Remove the chicken from the marinade (it should have taken on a reddish hue). Season both sides of the chicken breasts with a fair amount of salt and pepper. Lay the chicken on the hot grill, and sear for 8 minutes, rotating them halfway through cooking to "mark" them. Turn the chicken over and grill the other side for 6 more minutes. Remove the chicken to a cutting board. Using 2 forks, shred the chicken while it is still hot.

CHINESE FIVE-SPICE POWDER

A fragrant blend of star anise, cinnamon, clove, fennel and black pepper, five-spice powder brings a distinct, warm-sweet flavor to dishes. Chinese cooks prize five spice for the alluring flavor it lends to braised meats, poultry, and barbecued dishes. A little bit goes a long way, so use sparingly.

TANDOORI CHICKEN

SERVES 4

L.A. is a melting pot of food cultures and we're lucky to have some stellar Indian places around town. The warm, aromatic blend of spices is essential to traditional Indian cooking. It gives the chicken a sweet, smoky kick, which mimics the spirit of true tandoori. A great do-ahead recipes, marinate the chicken the day before and once cooked, the roasted pieces are delicious hot or cold.

1 tablespoon granulated garlic
1 tablespoon light brown sugar
1 tablespoon ground ginger
2 teaspoons ground cumin
2 teaspoons ground coriander
2 teaspoons paprika
2 teaspoons turmeric
2 teaspoons coarse salt
2 teaspoons cayenne pepper
2 tablespoons canola oil, plus
   2 more tablespoons
Juice of 1 lemon
4 (6-ounce) skinless boneless,
   chicken breast halves

IN A SMALL BOWL, combine the granulated garlic, sugar, ginger, cumin, coriander, paprika, turmeric, coarse salt, and cayenne pepper. Add 2 tablespoons of the oil and the lemon juice, stir with a spoon to form a thick paste. Rub all sides of the chicken with the tandoori paste, cover, and set aside in the refrigerator to marinate for at least 8 hours, preferably up to 24.

WHEN READY TO COOK THE CHICKEN, PREHEAT THE OVEN TO 400 DEGREES F.

PUT A CAST-IRON OR OVENPROOF SKILLET OVER MEDIUM-HIGH HEAT. Coat the pan with the remaining 2 tablespoons of oil. Once the oil is shimmering, lay the chicken in the pan—you may have to do this in batches. Sear each side for 3 minutes. Transfer the skillet (and chicken) to the oven and roast for roughly 15 minutes, or until cooked through.

MISO SALMON

SERVES 4

Salty, slightly sweet, and damn delicious, the contrasting flavors of this Miso Salmon dish complement one another. A touch of sesame oil provides fat (unsaturated, the good kind), orange contributes the acid that unlocks the salmon's flavor, miso gives a hint of salt, and rice vinegar adds a gentle sweetness.

¼ cup white miso (fermented soybean paste)

Juice of 1 orange (about ½ cup)

2 tablespoons seasoned rice vinegar

½ cup vegetable broth

1 tablespoon sesame oil

1 tablespoon light brown sugar, packed

1 scallion, white and green parts, thinly sliced

2 garlic cloves, minced

1-inch piece of ginger, peeled and minced

2 teaspoons ground ginger

½ teaspoon turmeric

½ teaspoon coarse salt

¼ teaspoon cayenne pepper

4 (5-ounce) wild salmon fillets, skin removed

2 tablespoons unsalted butter

IN A SMALL BOWL, whisk together the miso, orange juice, vinegar, broth, sesame oil, sugar, scallion, garlic, fresh and ground ginger, turmeric, salt, and cayenne. Place the salmon in a single layer in a baking dish or container. Pour the marinade over the fish, and turn to coat. Cover and chill at least 30 minutes or up to 2 hours.

PREHEAT THE BROILER. Line a large baking pan with aluminum foil. Remove the salmon fillets from the miso marinade and place side-by-side on the baking pan. Pour the marinade into a small pot and place over medium heat. Simmer the marinade until reduced by half into a sauce, about 2 minutes. Swirl the butter into the miso sauce and keep warm. Broil the salmon until the top is opaque and pink in the center, about 8 minutes. Drizzle the sauce over the salmon before serving.

CITRUS-POACHED SALMON, MUSTARD SAUCE

SERVES 4

Poaching fish is an easy, healthy way to get dinner on the table in a flash. This bright, tangy citrus broth made with orange, lemon, lime, dill, and white wine enhances the forward flavor of the salmon, and also doubles as the base for the mustard sauce. The poached salmon also makes a terrific salad for a hearty sandwich (page 164).

2 cups vegetable broth or water
½ cup dry white wine, such as
   Sauvignon Blanc
Juice of 1 seedless orange, plus
   3 slices
Juice of 1 lemon, plus 3 slices
Juice of 1 lime, plus 3 slices
2 garlic cloves
2 fresh dill sprigs, plus 1 tablespoon
   chopped
1 teaspoon whole black peppercorns
4 (5-ounce) wild salmon fillets,
   skin removed
Coarse salt
Freshly ground black pepper
1 tablespoon unsalted butter
1 tablespoon whole-grain Dijon
   mustard
1½ teaspoons smooth Dijon mustard
1 teaspoon honey or agave nectar

TO PREPARE THE POACHING LIQUID FOR THE SALMON, pour the broth and wine into a wide, shallow skillet or pot. Add the orange, lemon, and lime juices, the sliced citrus, garlic, dill sprigs, and peppercorns. Cover the pan and bring the liquid to a full boil over medium-high heat. You want to let the flavors of the aromatics infuse into the liquid. Once it comes to a boil, reduce the heat to medium-low and continue to simmer gently for about 15 minutes.

SEASON THE SALMON GENEROUSLY WITH SALT AND PEPPER. Lay the fillets in the pan (the liquid should come up halfway), cover, and simmer over medium-low heat until the salmon is barely opaque in the center, about 6 to 8 minutes. Take care to ensure that the liquid never gets hot enough to boil. Remove the salmon to a side plate.

TO PREPARE THE MUSTARD SAUCE, pour 1 cup of the poaching liquid into a small pot, discarding the rest. Simmer over medium heat to reduce the liquid by half. Whisk in the butter, whole grain and smooth mustards, honey, and chopped dill; season with salt and pepper if needed. Pour the mustard sauce over the fish before serving.

SHRIMP LOUIE, SRIRACHA AIOLI

SERVES 4

Although not a true Louie from San Francisco, this spicy shrimp salad sports its own L.A. style. The mayo's richness is boldly balanced with the heat of Sriracha and the vibrancy of lime and cilantro. Quick-pickled cucumber lends just the right amount of crunch and sweetness, and succulent avocado along with acidic grapefruit set off the subtle taste and texture of the shrimp. Try the Shrimp Louie on a toasted hot dog bun for a modern take on a New England lobster roll. The Sriracha Aioli makes a delicious spread for a tuna sandwich (page 163) or as a dip for French fries.

As with all cold preparations, the ingredients should be cold to start. Also take the time to chill your serving bowls to ensure the dish is enjoyed at the proper temperature.

1 hothouse cucumber, ends trimmed,
    halved lengthwise, and seeds
    scooped out with a spoon
2 teaspoons coarse salt
½ cup seasoned rice wine vinegar
¼ cup water
2 tablespoons sugar

SRIRACHA AIOLI
½ cup mayonnaise
1 to 2 tablespoons Sriracha hot sauce
½ teaspoon sesame oil
Juice of ½ lime
1 tablespoon finely chopped cilantro

SANDWICH
½ pound cooked small shrimp,
    such as Rock or Bay
4 firm-ripe Hass avocados, halved
    and pitted
1 small seedless grapefruit,
    segmented (see page 101)

DICE THE CUCUMBER INTO SMALL PIECES or shred with the large holes of a box grater. Mix the cucumber pieces in a strainer with the salt, and let stand in the sink or over a bowl for about 30 minutes, shaking and turning them a few times to drain their water. In the meantime, prepare the pickling liquid by combining the vinegar, water, and sugar in a small pot over medium heat. Bring the liquid to a boil, stirring to be sure the sugar dissolves, about 3 minutes. Remove from the heat and set aside in the refrigerator to chill.

AFTER THE CUCUMBERS DRAIN, squeeze the pieces in a dish towel to get out most of the liquid, and transfer them to a large bowl. Pour the chilled pickling liquid over the cucumbers, mixing well so all the pieces are coated. Set aside in the refrigerator for 1 hour. Drain the cucumbers from the liquid before adding to the salad.

TO PREPARE THE SRIRACHA AIOLI, combine the mayonnaise, Sriracha, sesame oil, lime, and cilantro in a mixing bowl. Blend well with a small whisk to fully incorporate the ingredients into the mayo.

ADD THE SHRIMP AND DRAINED CUCUMBERS to the Sriracha aioli; mix really well to coat in the mayo.

TO SERVE, mound the shrimp salad inside the avocado halves. Shingle a couple grapefruit segments on top to garnish. Serve 2 halves per person.

SEGMENTING CITRUS

To segment grapefruit (or orange, lemon, or lime for that matter), first trim the top and bottom flat so it stands steady on a work surface; cut deep enough so you see the meat of the fruit. Using a paring knife, cut off the skin and bitter white pith of the grapefruit, following the natural shape and turning as you do so. Trim off any white areas that remain. Hold the grapefruit over a bowl to catch their citrus juices. Carefully cut along the membrane, on both sides of each segment to free the pieces, and let them drop into the bowl. Then squeeze the segmented grapefruit over the wedges in the bowl to extract the remaining juice. Remove any seeds if necessary.

SEARED AHI TUNA,
CRUSHED ORANGE PONZU SAUCE

SERVES 4, MAKES 2 CUPS SAUCE

Make sure the hood in your kitchen is working before trying this recipe at home. The pan must be smoking hot and it's best to work quickly to get the tuna in, flipped, and out of the pan before potentially overcooking. Ponzu is a bracing accompaniment that cuts the dense richness of the fish. Crushed up orange wedge, skin and pith included, bulks up a typically thin Japanese sauce. The vibrant combination of peppery tuna and acidic orange sauce is both bold and light at the same time.

CRUSHED ORANGE PONZU

¼ small seedless orange, coarsely chopped (skin, pith, fruit, and all)

½ cup seasoned rice wine vinegar

2 tablespoons soy sauce

2 tablespoons honey or agave nectar

1 tablespoon ground ginger

1 tablespoon sesame oil

½ cup canola oil

1 Roma (plum) tomato, halved, seeded, and diced small

1 small shallot, minced

2 tablespoons finely chopped fresh chives

1 tablespoon sesame seeds, toasted

TUNA

1 tablespoon freshly ground black pepper

1½ teaspoons coarse salt

4 (5-ounce) sushi-quality tuna steaks (¾ to 1-inch thick)

2 tablespoons canola oil

TO PREPARE THE PONZU, in a blender combine the orange, vinegar, soy, honey, ginger, and sesame and canola oils. Blend on high speed until the orange is broken down but still a little bit chunky, about 1 minute. Pour the ponzu into a bowl, add the chopped tomato, shallot, chives, and sesame seeds, stirring to combine. Set aside while preparing the tuna to allow the flavors to come together.

TO PREPARE THE TUNA, in a small bowl, combine the pepper and salt, mixing with your fingers to evenly distribute. Pat the tuna dry with paper towels and sprinkle all sides with the salt and pepper mixture—you should see the seasoning on the tuna. Place a skillet over medium-high heat and coat with the oil. When the oil is hot, lay the tuna in the pan and sear for about 2 minutes on each side; as the tuna cooks, the red meat will become whiter and form a crust. Take care to move the fish as little as possible to minimize sticking and to avoid tearing the flesh.

REMOVE THE TUNA TO A CUTTING BOARD and cut on the diagonal into ¼-inch thick slices. Serve the tuna with the sauce spooned over the top.

GRILLED SKIRT STEAK, HOUSE STEAK SAUCE

SERVES 4, MAKES 1 CUP SAUCE

Skirt steak is one of my favorite cuts of meat and amazing on the grill. I think Worcestershire has incredible potential but find the regular store-bought sauce too thin to truly complement a great piece of meat, in this case skirt steak. So what I've done is fortify the bottled stuff with ketchup and other ingredients to create a thicker, richer version.

HOUSE STEAK SAUCE

1 tablespoon canola oil
1 small onion, coarsely chopped
2 garlic cloves, coarsely chopped
¼ cup fresh flat-leaf parsley, coarsely
    chopped
½ cup organic ketchup
½ cup vegetable broth or water
2 tablespoons Worcestershire sauce
1 tablespoon instant coffee
½ teaspoon coarse salt
1 teaspoon freshly ground black
    pepper

STEAK

2 pounds skirt steak
2 teaspoons chili powder
2 teaspoons coarse salt
1 teaspoon freshly ground black
    pepper

TO PREPARE THE SAUCE, place a 2-quart pot over medium heat and coat with the oil. When the oil is hot, add the onion, garlic, and parsley; cook, stirring, for a couple of minutes to soften. Add the Worcestershire, broth, ketchup, and coffee; season with salt and pepper. Reduce the heat to low, cover, and simmer for 20 minutes, until everything is soft. Puree with an immersion blender or carefully transfer to a standard blender. Serve hot or at room temperature with the steak. Store covered in the fridge for up to 2 weeks.

TO PREPARE THE STEAK, lay the skirt steak flat on a baking pan and season evenly on both sides with chili powder, salt, and pepper. Set aside at room temperature so the flavors can sink in a bit.

PREHEAT AN OUTDOOR GRILL OR GRILL PAN TO HIGH HEAT. Rub the grill with oil to prevent sticking. If you are using a grill pan, you may need to cut the steak in half and work in batches so it fits in the pan. Lay the steak on the grill and cook, turning with tongs from time to time, to sear well on all sides; this takes about 8 minutes total for medium-rare.

TRANSFER THE STEAK TO A CUTTING BOARD and let rest for 2 or 3 minutes to allow the juices to recirculate. Cut the skirt steak into thin slices *against the grain,* ensuring tenderness. Serve the steak with the steak sauce.

BRAISES

CLOSE YOUR EYES FOR A SECOND AND IMAGINE THE AROMA OF A POT OF *BBQ BRISKET* (page 110) wafting through the house. Slow braised for hours, the rich soft texture of practically melted beef makes this dish a timeless classic. This chapter is dedicated to good old-fashioned comfort food slow-simmered in big tightly covered pot—preferably a Dutch oven. Braising is about taking hefty cuts of meat, (like beef short ribs and pork belly), and layering flavors through aromatics and time; letting everything simmer peacefully until tender and intensely flavored.

While the cooking method remains basically the same throughout the recipes, they play around with international flavors like *Red Miso Beef, Lamb Tagine,* and *Green Curry Chicken* (pages 113, 120, 127). For the non-meat eater, the soul-satisfying *Vegetable Cook Pot* (page 134) is not to be missed!

Give yourself a long weekend afternoon to make these hearty braised dishes. Trust, the aromas will drive you crazy, but your patience and restraint will be amply rewarded come dinnertime. Most of these recipes also make plenty of leftovers featured in POT ROAST SANDWICHES (pages 136–149). As with all of the braises in this chapter, the flavors always improve if made ahead and reheated, which makes these dishes the perfect choice for entertaining.

TRADITIONAL BEEF SHORT RIB

SERVES 8 TO 10 (MAKES 10 CUPS)

The most back-to-basics of braises, this satisfying Sunday supper is sure to be a welcome addition to your cooking arsenal. Make your life easy and have the guy at the meat counter take the rib bones out of the beef for you. Short ribs need slow, moist cooking. Leftovers transform into a country-style sandwich adorned with decadent Mac 'n Cheese (page 179).

5 pounds boneless beef short ribs, patted dry
Coarse salt
Freshly ground black pepper
2 tablespoons canola oil
1 onion, coarsely chopped
2 celery stalks, coarsely chopped
2 carrots, coarsely chopped
2 garlic cloves, coarsely chopped
4 fresh thyme sprigs
1 cup balsamic vinegar
1 cup red wine vinegar
2 quarts low-sodium chicken broth
¼ cup freshly grated or jarred horseradish
2 big handfuls fresh flat-leaf parsley, coarsely chopped

SEASON THE SHORT RIBS GENEROUSLY WITH SALT AND PEPPER. Put a large, wide Dutch oven or pot over medium-high heat and coat with the oil. When the oil is hot, lay the ribs in the pot in a single layer; do this in batches so you don't overcrowd the pot. Brown the meat well on all sides, turning with tongs. It will take about 30 minutes. When the ribs are nicely browned, transfer to a side plate.

TURN THE HEAT DOWN TO MEDIUM. Add the onion, carrot, celery, garlic, and thyme. Stir with a wooden spoon, scraping up all the crusty bits in the pan. Cook for 6 to 8 minutes, until the vegetables just begin to get some color. Pour in the balsamic and red wine vinegars. Turn the heat up to high and reduce the liquid by half; about 10 minutes.

STIR IN THE BROTH, horseradish, and parsley and bring to a boil. Return the short ribs to the pot, along with any accumulated juices. The stock mixture should almost cover the ribs. Cover and reduce the heat to low. Braise until the meat is very tender, about 3½ hours.

REMOVE THE LID AND PIERCE A SHORT RIB with a paring knife; it will fall apart. If you would like to cook these a day ahead, this is where you can pause.

TRANSFER THE SHORT RIBS TO A LARGE PLATTER, removing the excess vegetables. Then pass the braising liquid through a large strainer into a large measuring cup, spoon off the excess fat that rises to the surface, and then add the liquid back to the meat. If serving the short ribs for Beef Stroganoff (page 000), let the meat cool in the braising liquid.

BBQ BRISKET

SERVES 6 TO 8 (MAKES 8 CUPS), MAKES 1 QUART SAUCE

Brisket is a relatively tough piece of meat, but with a penetrating marinade and a slow-and-steady cooking process, the beef becomes fork-tender, juicy, and dripping with flavor. Using cola in barbecue sauce is a long-standing tradition in the South that adds a touch of effervescence and infuses a concentrated amber sweetness. This chunky, hearty, braised beef is the ultimate comfort food and smells like home no matter where you're from. Serve with Green Tomato, Sweet Corn, Pepita, Ancho Chili Vinaigrette (page 12) and your favorite Lemonade (pages 225–234).

1 tablespoon granulated onion
1 tablespoon ground cumin
1 tablespoon light brown sugar
2 teaspoons chili powder
2 teaspoons coarse salt
1 teaspoon freshly ground black
   pepper
1 (4-pound) beef brisket, first-cut,
   cut into 3-inch chunks
2 tablespoons canola oil
2 tablespoons unsalted butter
1 small onion, chopped
4 garlic cloves, chopped
2 tablespoons tomato paste
1 (20-ounce) bottle cola
1 (28-ounce) can chopped tomatoes
¼ cup apple cider vinegar
¼ cup balsamic vinegar
2 tablespoons Worcestershire sauce
2 tablespoons Dijon mustard
2 tablespoons hot sauce, such as
   Tabasco sauce
2 tablespoons light brown sugar
1 tablespoon barbecue spice, such
   as McCormick or Frontier

IN A SMALL BOWL, combine the granulated onion, cumin, sugar, chili powder, salt, and pepper; toss with your fingers to mix. Rub the spice mixture on all sides of the brisket cubes. If you have time, wrap the brisket in plastic and let it cure, in the refrigerator, for 4 to 8 hours (or even overnight). Don't worry if you don't have time for this—the meat will still be plenty flavorful, even if you only have 30 minutes.

PUT A LARGE, WIDE DUTCH OVEN OR pot over medium-high heat and coat with the oil. When the oil is hot, lay the brisket in the pot in a single layer; do this in batches so you don't over-crowd. Brown the meat well on all sides, turning with tongs. Transfer the meat to a side plate and repeat with the remaining chunks. Carefully discard about half the fat from the pot, then add the butter, onion, garlic, and tomato paste. Cook, stirring, over medium heat until browned and tender, about 4 minutes.

POUR IN THE COLA AND COOK, stirring occasionally, until reduced by about half. Add the crushed tomatoes, apple cider and balsamic vinegars, Worcestershire, mustard, hot sauce, sugar, and spice. Stir everything together to combine and bring to a boil. Nestle the brisket chunks back into the pot, cover, and reduce the heat to medium-low. Simmer for 3½ hours until the meat is fork tender and the barbecue sauce is thick.

RED MISO BEEF

This beautiful beef braise is a concoction of Texas barbecue, Mexican molé, and Japanese miso soup. While not being "true" to any one ethnicity, integrating culturally diverse ingredients is very Californian in its open approach to mingling flavors to create something out of the ordinary. Glossy in it's brick red–colored sauce and flecked with ginger and sesame, the layers of distinctive flavors make this dish difficult to stop eating; the salty-sweet red miso, fiery red chili, allspice, molasses, and vinegar all come through. Serve over steamed rice.

5 pounds boneless beef short ribs, patted dry
Coarse salt
Freshly ground black pepper
2 tablespoons canola oil
1 onion, chopped
4 scallions, white and green parts, chopped
4 garlic cloves, chopped
1 (1-inch) piece fresh ginger, peeled and chopped
1 tablespoon sesame seeds
1 tablespoon allspice
½ cup apple cider vinegar
½ cup ketchup
½ cup molasses
½ cup red miso paste (fermented soybean paste)
2 tablespoons Sambal Oelek chili paste (see page 31)
2 tablespoons Dijon mustard
2 cups low-sodium beef broth

SEASON THE SHORT RIBS generously with salt and pepper; you should be able to see the seasoning on the meat.

PLACE A LARGE, WIDE DUTCH OVEN or pot over medium-high heat and coat with the oil. When the oil is hot, lay the short ribs in the pot in a single layer; do this in batches so you don't overcrowd the pot. Brown the meat well on all sides, turning with tongs. Do not rush this step; it will take about 30 minutes. When the ribs are nicely browned, transfer them to a side plate.

TURN THE HEAT DOWN TO MEDIUM. Add the onion, scallions, garlic, ginger, sesame seeds, and allspice. Stir with a wooden spoon and cook for 4 to 6 minutes, until fragrant and tender. Add the vinegar, turn the heat up to high, and reduce the liquid by half; this should take about 2 minutes.

STIR IN THE KETCHUP, MOLASSES, MISO PASTE, CHILI PASTE, mustard, and broth and bring to a boil. Return the short ribs to the pot, along with any accumulated juices. The stock mixture should almost cover the ribs. Cover and reduce the heat to low. Braise until the meat is very tender, about 3½ hours.

BEEF STROGANOFF

Some recipes age well, evoking memories of simpler times, and Stroganoff is a definite throwback to my childhood. Every Monday night, my twelve cousins and I would gather for supper in my grandmother Susie's kitchen, wafting with the smell of stewed meat and noodles at the door. This updated family classic gets striped down to bare essentials L.A. style. To grandmother's house we go!

3 tablespoons unsalted butter

1 onion, diced

8 ounces button mushrooms (3 cups), wiped of grit, stemmed, and halved if large

Coarse salt and freshly ground black pepper

1 tablespoon paprika

¼ cup tomato paste

2 cups tomato puree

1 quart Traditional Beef Short Rib braising liquid (see page 109), or low-sodium beef broth

1 pound Traditional Beef Short Rib (see page 109), shredded (about 3½ cups)

2 tablespoons all-purpose flour

½ cup sour cream

½ bunch fresh flat-leaf parsley, chopped

Cooked buttered egg noodles, for serving

PLACE A 3-QUART POT OVER MEDIUM HEAT and add 2 tablespoons of the butter. When the butter has melted, toss in the onion and mushrooms. Cook and stir until the vegetables lose their moisture and begin to brown, about 5 minutes. Season with salt, pepper, and paprika.

STIR IN THE TOMATO PASTE AND PUREE. Pour in the braising liquid and simmer, uncovered, until the liquid cooks down and thickens slightly, about 10 minutes. Fold the beef into the liquid and continue to cook until heated through.

ROLL THE REMAINING 1 TABLESPOON OF BUTTER IN THE FLOUR and whisk into the sauce, taking care to smooth out any lumps. Cook and stir until the sauce thickens. Remove from the heat and stir in the sour cream. Shower the top with parsley. Serve with buttered egg noodles.

BRAISED PORK BELLY

SERVES 4 TO 6

Let's be clear, this dish takes a bit of time to make . . . but the result is so well worth it! Succulent (code for fatty), pork belly gets the royal treatment and withstands three cooking processes—brining, braising, and searing—to produce the most delicious morsels of meat imaginable. In L.A., pork belly has no boundaries and appears on menus across the board—from food trucks to fine dining. Scatter pork belly over pizza or stuff into a hunky sandwich (page 139).

PORK BELLY

1 quart water

¼ cup sugar

2½ tablespoons coarse salt

2 bay leaves, preferably fresh

3 garlic cloves, smashed

1 teaspoon red pepper flakes

3 pounds pork belly, excess fat trimmed and scored

Coarse salt

Freshly ground black pepper

2 tablespoons canola oil

1 yellow onion, coarsely chopped

6 garlic cloves, coarsely chopped

½ bunch fresh thyme sprigs, coarsely chopped

½ bunch fresh flat-leaf parsley sprigs, coarsely chopped

1 tablespoon whole black peppercorns

1 cup dry white wine, such as *Sauvignon Blanc*

1 quart low-sodium chicken broth

TO PREPARE THE PORK BRINE, combine the water, sugar, salt, bay leaves, garlic, and red pepper flakes in a gallon size plastic bag. Give the mixture a few good stirs to dissolve the sugar and salt. Submerge the pork belly in the brine, seal up the bag, pressing out the air, and put it in the refrigerator for 8 hours or overnight to tenderize the meat. Remove the pork belly from the brine and pat dry with paper towels. Discard the brine.

TO BRAISE THE PORK, season both sides of the meat heavily with salt and pepper. Place a large Dutch oven or deep ovenproof pot over medium heat and coat with 1 tablespoon of the oil. When the oil gets hot, lay the pork belly in the pan and sear for 6 minutes on each side, turning once, until the fat begins to render and crisp and the meat is brown.

REMOVE THE SEARED PORK BELLY to a side platter and carefully pour out all but 2 tablespoons of the rendered fat. To the drippings, add the onion, garlic, thyme, parsley, and peppercorns. Sweat the vegetables in the pork fat, cook and stir often, until soft, about 15 minutes.

PREHEAT THE OVEN TO 375 DEGREES F.

POUR IN THE WINE, stirring to scrape the bits on the bottom of the pot, and continue to cook for 5 minutes, until the liquid is reduced and looks syrupy. Turn the heat up to high, pour in the broth, and bring to a boil.

Continued on next page

RETURN THE SEARED PORK BELLY TO THE POT; the liquid should just barely cover the meat. Cover with a lid and transfer to the hot oven and braise until the pork is very tender and a fork slides into the meat without any resistance, about 2½ hours.

ALLOW THE PORK BELLY TO COOL COMPLETELY IN THE BRAISING LIQUID at room temperature. This is a great thing to get out of the way a day or 2 before you want to serve. Store the pork in the fridge submerged in the braising liquid and covered. Remove the cooled pork from the liquid and pat dry with paper towels to eliminate excess moisture and any solidified fat from the surface of the meat.

USING A SHARP KNIFE, DIVIDE THE PORK INTO 4 EQUAL PORTIONS; it is easier to cut when the meat is cool. Season the pieces of pork belly generously with salt and pepper. Place a cast-iron skillet or deep ovenproof pan over medium heat and coat with the remaining 1 tablespoon of oil. When the oil is hot, lay the pork belly in the pan, fat-side down. Sear for 3 minutes until the fat forms a really crispy crust. Turn the pork over and cook the other side for another 2 minutes to brown the meat. Cut the belly crosswise into ½-inch-thick strips.

PORK BELLY

Pork belly, which comes from the underside of the hog, is basically uncured fresh bacon. The rosy meat is marbled with fat and when brined, braised, and seared (as it is here), the pork becomes custardy soft and you can literally cut it with a spoon. I have to say; the succulent and crackling fat is what makes it taste so damn delicious! A good butcher should be able to help you out when buying pork belly and it's typically an inexpensive cut. Ask for unsalted, uncured belly, which is not the same as a slab bacon or salt pork. You can often find pork belly in Asian markets, as it is used a lot in their cuisine.

JACKSON'S PULLED PORK, BARBECUE SAUCE

SERVES 6 TO 8 (MAKES 8 CUPS)

Pulled Pork is a real crowd pleaser, making this dish a solid choice for a casual family-style supper. This also makes delectable moist and tender sandwiches topped with slaw.

PULLED PORK
¼ cup Ancho chili powder
    (see page 13)
2 tablespoons paprika
2 tablespoons light brown sugar
2 tablespoons ground coriander
1 tablespoon granulated onion
1 tablespoon coarse salt
1 teaspoon freshly ground black
    pepper
1 (4-pound) boneless pork butt,
    cut into 3-inch chunks
2 tablespoons canola oil
1 quart low-sodium chicken or
    beef broth

BARBECUE SAUCE
1 tablespoon canola oil
1 onion, chopped
2 garlic cloves, chopped
1 cup ketchup
¼ cup Worcestershire sauce
¼ cup red wine vinegar
2 tablespoons honey
1 teaspoon dry mustard

Makes 1½ cups

IN A SMALL BOWL, combine the chili powder, paprika, sugar, coriander, granulated onion, salt, and pepper; toss with your fingers to incorporate the ingredients. Rub the spice mixture on the pork chunks. If you have time, wrap the pork in plastic in the refrigerator, for 4 to 8 hours (or even overnight), but don't worry if you don't have time for this—the meat will be plenty flavorful, even if you cook it right away.

PLACE A LARGE DUTCH OVEN or pot over medium-high heat and coat with the oil. When hot, lay the pork in the pot in a single layer; do this in batches so you don't overcrowd the pot. Brown the meat well on all sides. Transfer the meat to a side plate and repeat. Carefully discard about half the fat from the pot. Turn the heat up to high, pour in the broth, and bring to a boil.

RETURN THE SEARED PORK TO THE POT; the liquid should just barely cover the meat. Cover and transfer to the hot oven and braise until the pork is very tender and a fork slides into the meat without any resistance, about 2½ hours. Basically, you want to braise the pork until it's falling apart and an instant-read thermometer inserted into the thickest part registers 170 degrees F.

REMOVE THE PORK CHUNKS TO A CUTTING BOARD. Allow the meat to rest for about 10 minutes. While still warm, take 2 forks and "pull" the meat to form shreds. Set aside.

TO MAKE THE BARBECUE SAUCE, put a 2-quart pot over medium heat and coat with the oil. When the oil is hot, add the onion and garlic. Cook until the onion is soft, about 2 minutes. Add the ketchup, Worcestershire, vinegar, honey, and mustard. Reduce the heat to medium-low, cover, and gently simmer for 15 minutes until the sugar dissolves, stirring occasionally. Uncover and add the shredded pork to the sauce, mixing to combine. Simmer for another 5 minutes to warm through.

LAMB TAGINE, FIGS, APRICOTS, ALMONDS

SERVES 4 TO 6 (MAKES 6 CUPS)

Call it a braise, stew, or tagine, this slow-simmered lamb dish gets its Moroccan flair from a blend of aromatic spices such as turmeric, cumin, ginger, allspice, and cinnamon. Studded with plumped-up dried fruit and finished with crunchy almonds, this earthy lamb stew is a winning combination of sweet and savory. As a main coarse, serve with Rice Pilaf, Nectarine, White Cheddar, Mint Vinaigrette (page 64) or couscous. Leftover lamb tagine makes a decadent panini sandwich laden with feta cheese and arugula (page 149).

SPICE MIX

2 tablespoons curry powder, preferably Madras

2 tablespoons ground ginger

2 tablespoons light brown sugar, packed

1 tablespoon ground cumin

2 teaspoons turmeric

2 teaspoons allspice

2 teaspoons coarse salt

1 teaspoon ground cinnamon

1 teaspoon cayenne pepper

1 teaspoon freshly ground black pepper

LAMB STEW

3 tablespoons canola oil

3 pounds boneless leg of lamb, trimmed of excess fat, cut into 1-inch cubes

1 onion, finely chopped

1 carrot, finely chopped

1 celery stalk, finely chopped

1 quart low-sodium chicken broth

½ cup dried apricots, sliced

½ cup dried Mission figs, sliced

½ cup slivered almonds, toasted (see page 3)

Juice of ½ lemon

2 big handfuls each fresh cilantro and mint, chopped, for garnish

MAKE THE SPICE MIX BY COMBINING the curry, ginger, sugar, cumin, turmeric, allspice, salt, cinnamon, cayenne, and pepper in a small bowl. Toss with your fingers to evenly distribute the ingredients.

PUT THE LAMB IN A MIXING BOWL. Season the lamb generously with spice mix and toss thoroughly to coat completely. If you have time, cover and marinate for 30 minutes so the flavors can sink into the meat a bit.

PLACE A LARGE, WIDE DUTCH OVEN or pot over medium-high heat and coat with the oil. When the oil is hot, lay the lamb in the pot in a single layer; do this in batches so you don't overcrowd the pot. Brown the meat well on all sides, turning with tongs. Do not rush this step; it will take about 20 minutes. When the lamb is nicely browned, transfer to a plate. Add the onion, carrot, and celery to the drippings in the pot, stirring occasionally until fragrant, about 3 minutes. Return the lamb to the pot and pour in the broth. Bring to a simmer, cover, and cook over low heat for 45 minutes.

ADD THE APRICOTS, FIGS, AND ALMONDS; give a squeeze of lemon juice to brighten up the flavor. Stir everything together, cover, reduce the heat to low, and simmer for roughly another 30 minutes; stirring occasionally. Shower with cilantro and mint before serving.

CHICKEN BASQUE,
OLIVES, ARTICHOKES

SERVES 4 TO 6 (MAKES 6 CUPS)

A departure from rustic chicken fricassee, this Mediterranean one-pot wonder is a little bit unusual but not difficult to make in the slightest bit. Moist dark meat chicken is nestled in a thick, colorful medley of tomatoes, bell pepper, olives, and artichokes. This abundant stew should make a little extra for leftovers, which are even better in a hearty sandwich crowned with melted Manchego cheese (page 146)!

4 pounds chicken thighs (about 12), skinless, bone-in
2 teaspoons coarse salt, plus more for seasoning
1 teaspoon freshly ground black pepper, plus more for seasoning
1 teaspoon paprika
½ cup all-purpose flour
¼ cup canola oil
1 medium white onion, large dice
4 garlic cloves, minced
1 red bell pepper, stemmed, halved, cored, seeded, and chopped
¼ cup sherry vinegar
24 pitted green olives, such as Manzanilla (about ½ cup)
24 pitted Kalamata olives (about ½ cup)
2 (4-ounce) jars artichoke hearts in water, drained, rinsed, and quartered
4 plum (Roma) tomatoes, halved, seeded, and diced
1 quart low-sodium chicken broth
Lemon wedges, for serving

PREHEAT THE OVEN TO 375 DEGREES F.

SEASON THE CHICKEN LIBERALLY with 1 teaspoon salt, ½ teaspoon pepper, and paprika. Spread the flour in a large shallow platter. Dredge the chicken lightly in the flour to coat all sides, tapping off the excess.

PUT A LARGE, WIDE DUTCH OVEN or pot over medium-high heat and coat with the oil. When the oil is hot, add half of the chicken and brown for 4 to 5 minutes on each side, without moving the pieces around too much so you get a good sear. Remove the browned chicken to a platter and repeat with the remaining chicken thighs, removing them to the platter when done.

TO THE DRIPPINGS IN THE POT, add the onion, garlic, and bell pepper. Cook and stir for about 3 minutes, or until the vegetables soften and begin to get some color. Pour in the vinegar stirring to scrape up the brown bits in the bottom of the pot. Add the olives, artichokes, tomatoes, and broth. Nestle the chicken back in the pot, along with any accumulated juices, so the thighs are covered with the olives and stuff, season with salt and pepper.

BRING THE STEW TO A BOIL, cover, and transfer to the oven. Bake for 1 to 1½ hours, or until your kitchen smells amazing. Garnish the chicken stew with lemon wedges before serving. Squeezing lemon onto the dish at the end is essential! That little bit of acid brings out all the flavors in the broth and balances out the richness of chicken thighs.

TURKEY, DRIED CRANBERRY, SAGE GRAVY

SERVES 8 TO 10 (MAKES 10 CUPS)

The union of turkey, cranberry, and sage naturally evokes all senses to Thanksgiving. For a sunny Southern California twist, I've incorporated an entire orange into the sage gravy to add sparkle to a holiday mainstay. This sassy, all in one braise, combines beloved cool-weather ingredients in a single pot without much fuss. Braising the skinless turkey adds deep poultry flavor throughout the dish, while cutting back on fat. The meat immerses moist and delicate.

1 cup all-purpose flour, plus
    2 tablespoons
2 teaspoons dried thyme
2 teaspoons coarse salt, plus more
    for seasoning
1 teaspoon freshly ground black
    pepper, plus more for seasoning
3 turkey legs (about 2 pounds),
    skinless
2 turkey thighs (about 2 pounds),
    skinless
2 tablespoons canola oil
1 tablespoon unsalted butter
1 onion, chopped
1 carrot, ends trimmed and chopped
1 celery stalk, ends trimmed and
    chopped
2 bay leaves
4 fresh thyme sprigs
1 cup orange juice
1 quart low-sodium chicken broth
1 seedless orange, sliced (skin, pith,
    fruit, and all)
4 fresh sage sprigs
1 cup dried cranberries

PREHEAT THE OVEN TO 375 DEGREES F.

SPREAD THE 2 CUPS OF FLOUR IN A LARGE SHALLOW PLATTER and add the dried thyme, 1 teaspoon salt, and 1 teaspoon pepper; mix with your fingers to incorporate. Dredge the turkey legs and thighs lightly in the seasoned flour to coat all sides, tapping off the excess.

PLACE A LARGE, WIDE DUTCH OVEN or pot over medium-high heat and add the butter and oil. When the butter is foamy, lay the turkey legs in the pot and brown for 6 to 8 minutes on each side, without moving the pieces around too much so you get a good sear. Remove the browned turkey legs to a platter and repeat with the turkey thighs, removing them to the platter when done.

ADD THE ONION, CARROT, CELERY, BAY LEAVES, AND FRESH THYME to the drippings in the pot. Turn the heat down to medium. Cook and stir for about 3 minutes, or until the vegetables soften and begin to get some color. Sprinkle in the remaining 2 tablespoons of flour, stirring to incorporate into the vegetables and cook out the raw taste. Pour in the orange juice and reduce the liquid by half; this should take about 3 minutes.

ADD THE BROTH, orange slices, and sage and bring to a boil. Nestle the turkey back in the pot, along with any accumulated juices; season with salt and pepper. The stock should almost cover the meat. Bring the stew to a boil, cover, and transfer to the oven. Bake the turkey for 1½ hours, or until your kitchen smells amazing.

REMOVE THE TURKEY FROM THE POT and set aside on a cutting board. Place the pot over medium-high heat. Add the dried cranberries to the broth. Simmer, uncovered, for another 15 minutes, stirring occasionally, to reduce and thicken into a sauce. Using a sharp knife, carve the turkey meat from the bones of the legs and thighs. Put the turkey slices in the gravy and stir to combine.

GREEN CURRY CHICKEN, COCONUT, LONG BEANS, THAI BASIL

SERVES 8 TO 10 (MAKES 10 CUPS)

If you love Thai food, this is an excellent dish to start playing around with. The floral aroma of Green Curry Chicken simmering on the stove is hypnotic! Lemongrass, coconut milk, ginger, basil, and lime round out the stew's intense flavor. While this green curry hot pot is fundamentally Thai-inspired, the Californian twist is the addition of Granny Smith apples and orange juice. Because this warm dish is so light, you can enjoy it year-round.

2 tablespoons canola oil

1 onion, cut into large chunks

2-inch piece fresh ginger, peeled and chopped (about 4 tablespoons)

2 lemongrass stalks, green tops removed, halved lengthwise and bulb smashed

½ teaspoon coarse salt

¼ teaspoon freshly ground black pepper

3 tablespoons Thai green curry paste

3 tablespoons light brown sugar

¼ cup mirin (Japanese sweet rice wine)

¼ cup orange juice

2 Granny Smith apples, cored and cut into large chunks (see page 9)

1 (14-ounce) can unsweetened coconut milk

1 quart low-sodium chicken broth

2 pounds skinless boneless chicken breast halves, cut into 1-inch chunks

1½ pounds Chinese long beans (about ½ bunch), cut into 2-inch pieces (see page 43)

1 cup fresh Thai basil leaves, hand-torn

Lime wedges, for serving

TO PREPARE THE CURRY SAUCE, place a large, wide Dutch oven or pot over medium-high heat and coat with the oil. When the oil is hot, add the onion, ginger, and lemongrass; season with salt and pepper. Cook and stir for 2 minutes until the vegetables are fragrant. Stir in the curry paste and brown sugar, mixing well to incorporate. Pour in the mirin and orange juice, stirring until almost completely evaporated, about 3 minutes.

ADD THE APPLES, COCONUT MILK, AND BROTH. Cover the pot and bring the liquid to a boil; you want to let the flavors of the aromatics infuse into the liquid. Once it comes to a boil, reduce the heat to medium-low and continue to gently simmer for about 15 minutes.

LAY THE CHICKEN CHUNKS IN THE COCONUT MILK SAUCE, cover, and simmer until the chicken is fully cooked, about 25 minutes. Uncover, remove the lemon grass, and add the long beans and basil. Simmer until the beans are just tender, about 5 minutes. Serve in dinner bowls with wedges of lime.

MOROCCAN CHICKEN, DATES, OLIVES

SERVES 6 TO 8 (MAKES 8 CUPS)

Similar to Los Angeles' cuisine, Moroccan food is known for its remarkable diversity of influences. You can trace the country's long history of colonizers and immigrants who have left their mark, especially in food. The essence of Moroccan cooking is a meld of spices like cumin and ginger, with local ingredients such as olives and dates. The enticing combination strikes a lively balance of sweet and savory.

1 tablespoon granulated garlic
1 tablespoon ground cumin
1 tablespoon light brown sugar
2 teaspoons ground ginger
2 teaspoons coarse salt, plus more
    for seasoning
1 teaspoon freshly ground black
    pepper, plus more for seasoning
4 chicken thighs, bone-in, skin on
4 chicken legs, bone-in, skin on
2 tablespoons canola oil
1 onion, chopped
2 garlic cloves, minced
1 red bell pepper, halved, seeded,
    and chopped
½-inch piece fresh ginger, peeled
    and chopped (about 1 tablespoon)
12 pitted green olives, such as
    Manzanilla (about ¼ cup)
12 pitted black olives, such as
    Kalamata (about ¼ cup)
12 dried dates
4 sprigs fresh thyme, leaves stripped
    from the stem
2 sprigs fresh oregano, leaves
    stripped from the stem
1 quart low-sodium chicken broth

IN A SMALL BOWL, combine the granulated garlic, cumin, sugar, ginger, salt, and pepper; toss with your fingers to mix. Rub the spice mixture on all sides of the chicken.

PLACE A LARGE, wide Dutch oven or pot over medium-high heat and coat with the oil. When the oil is hot, add half of the chicken and brown for 4 to 6 minutes on each side, without moving the pieces around too much so you get a good sear. Remove the browned chicken to a platter and repeat with the remaining chicken thighs, removing them to the platter when done.

TO THE DRIPPINGS IN THE POT, add the onion, garlic, and bell pepper. Cook and stir for about 5 minutes, or until the vegetables soften and begin to get some color. Add the ginger, olives, dates, thyme, oregano, and broth. Nestle the chicken back in the pot, along with any accumulated juices, so the pieces are covered with the olives and stuff; season with salt and pepper. Bring the stew to a boil, cover, and reduce to medium-low heat. Simmer for 45 minutes. Remove the lid and simmer for another 10 minutes to reduce the sauce until slightly thickened.

JAMAICAN JERK CHICKEN

SERVES 6 TO 8 (MAKES 8 CUPS)

Jamaican Jerk Chicken reminds me of the days as a teenager smoking clove cigarettes and jamming to ska band, The English Beat. When used too liberally, clove's robust flavor can run rampant over everything else. Using just a touch, though, adds a musky aroma to the chicken stew and rounds out the warm spice of ginger, allspice, nutmeg, and habañero. To cool off your palate, serve with Sweet Potato, Parsley, Pistachio Vinaigrette (page 20).

1 tablespoon ground ginger
1½ teaspoons allspice
1½ teaspoons coarse salt
1 teaspoon freshly ground black
   pepper
1 teaspoon ground cloves
1 teaspoon freshly ground nutmeg
6 chicken thighs, skinless, boneless
   (about 2 pounds)
2 tablespoons canola oil

SAUCE
2 tablespoons canola oil
1 onion, chopped
2 garlic cloves, chopped
½-inch piece fresh ginger, peeled
   and minced (about 1 tablespoon)
1 habañero, seeded and minced
½ cup light brown sugar, lightly
   packed
2 teaspoons dried thyme
1 teaspoon allspice
1 teaspoon freshly ground nutmeg
1 teaspoon ground ginger
1 tablespoon coarse salt
1 tablespoon freshly ground black
   pepper
3 cups low-sodium chicken broth
Juice of 1 lime

IN A SMALL BOWL, COMBINE the ginger, allspice, salt, pepper, clove, and nutmeg; mix with your fingers to evenly distribute the ingredients.

Rinse the chicken pieces in water and pat dry with paper towels. Arrange the chicken side-by-side on a baking pan and sprinkle the spice mix all over the chicken, turning to season all sides. Set aside for 10 minutes.

PREHEAT THE OVEN TO 400 DEGREES F.

DRIZZLE THE CHICKEN WITH 2 TABLESPOONS OF THE OIL, tossing to coat. Bake for 30 minutes until the chicken is golden and the meat is just about fully cooked. In the meantime, prepare the sauce.

TO PREPARE THE SAUCE, place a large, wide Dutch oven or pot over medium-high heat and coat with 2 tablespoons of oil. When the oil is hot, add the onion, garlic, fresh ginger, and habañero. Cook and stir for 2 minutes until the vegetables are fragrant. Lower the heat to medium-low, and add the sugar, dried thyme, allspice, nutmeg, ground ginger, salt, and pepper; stir constantly to be sure the spices don't burn. Pour in the broth, stirring to incorporate. Bring the sauce to a boil, cover, and reduce to medium-low heat. Cook, for about 10 minutes, until the sugar dissolves and the ingredients start to bubble.

Remove the chicken from the oven and lay the baked chicken pieces in the sauce, cover, and simmer until the chicken is fully cooked, about 15 minutes. Squeeze in the lime just before serving.

CHINESE-STYLE BRAISED DUCK

SERVES 4

Duck, the most succulent of birds, shines in this simple yet sophisticated recipe. With its assertive, meaty flavor it is an elegant alternative to chicken. Duck's rich, pronounced flavor is best accented with sharp ingredients like orange, ginger, and lemongrass. Cooking duck legs is not at all difficult, so if you've never cooked them before, give this recipe a shot. For a complete Asian meal, serve with Forbidden Rice, Heart of Palm, Mushroom, Jalapeño Vinaigrette (page 62), and Chinese Long Bean, Pluot Plum, Plum Vinaigrette (page 42).

4 large whole duck legs (about 2 pounds), trimmed of excess fat
Coarse salt and freshly ground black pepper
1 seedless orange, cut into large chunks (skin, pith, fruit, and all)
6 garlic cloves, smashed
2-inch piece fresh ginger, halved lengthwise and smashed
2 lemongrass stalks, green tops removed, bulb smashed
1 handful cilantro stems
1 tablespoon whole black peppercorns
1 tablespoon sesame oil
1 quart low-sodium chicken broth

PLACE A DUTCH OVEN or wide pot large enough to hold the duck legs in a single layer over medium-high heat. Season the duck legs generously with salt and pepper. Brown the duck legs, skin-side down, until the skin is crisp and dark brown, about 10 minutes.

PERIODICALLY SPOON OFF the rendered duck fat. Turn the legs over with tongs and brown the other side for about 2 minutes.

TOSS IN THE ORANGE, garlic, ginger, lemongrass, cilantro stems, and peppercorns. Pour in the sesame oil and broth. Reduce the heat to medium-low, cover, and braise the duck legs until tender, about 1 hour. Alternatively, you may bake in a 300 degree F. oven. Serve immediately or allow the duck to cool in the liquid at room temperature; this keeps the legs from drying out. The braised duck legs can easily be prepared in advance, covered, and refrigerated in the broth.

VEGETABLE COOK POT

SERVES 6 TO 8 (MAKES 8 CUPS)

Renowned chef Alain Ducasse features his signature vegetable dish called "cookpots" at his restaurants around the world. He deftly combines a harmonic blend of seasonal vegetables and then gently cooks them in a specially designed white porcelain-covered crock. This divine dish is a nod to Ducasse's simple philosophy of eating food from the earth aesthetic to showcase vegetables in their simplest form. Because the purity of this stew is in the vegetables, take a little extra time to make the homemade vegetable broth as directed in the recipe. Store-bought broth in cartons tends to have a muddy, yellowish tinge. The clear broth caresses the delicate vegetables, creating a light and almost medicinal meal.

VEGETABLE BROTH

½ onion, halved and sliced
½ fennel bulb, halved, cored,
   and sliced
1 celery stalk, chopped
2 garlic cloves
1½ teaspoons whole white
   peppercorns
1½ teaspoons whole black
   peppercorns
1½ teaspoons fennel seeds
1 bay leaf
1 cup dry white wine, such as
   Sauvignon Blanc
2 quarts water

SOUP

2 tablespoons canola oil
2 carrots, chopped
1-inch piece daikon radish, peeled,
   halved, and cut into ½-inch chunks
1 small turnip, peeled, halved, and cut
   into ½-inch chunks
1 celery root, peeled, halved,
   and cut into ½-inch chunks
2 parsnips, peeled, halved,
   and cut into ½-inch chunks
½ head Savoy cabbage, cored
   and cut crosswise into ribbons
1 Granny smith apple, cored and cut
   into chunks (see page 9)
1 teaspoon coarse salt
½ teaspoon freshly ground black
   pepper
¼ cup fresh flat-leaf parsley, chopped
Juice of 1 lemon
Extra-virgin olive oil, for serving

TO MAKE THE VEGETABLE BROTH, put the onion, fennel, celery, garlic, peppercorns, fennel seeds, bay leaves, wine, and water in a soup pot. Bring slowly up to a boil over medium-low heat; the goal is to gently extract as much flavor as possible out of the vegetables and spices into the liquid. Reduce to low and slowly simmer, uncovered, for 30 minutes; low and slow is the mantra. Skim any impurities that may rise to the surface during cooking.

TURN OFF THE HEAT and let the vegetable broth steep for 10 minutes and cool a bit. Strain the broth into another pot to remove the solids; don't press down on the ingredients, the broth should be clear, not cloudy.

TO PREPARE THE SOUP, put a large, wide Dutch oven or pot over medium-high heat and coat with the oil. When the oil is hot, add the carrots, daikon, turnip, celery root, and parsnips. Cook and stir for 5 minutes until the vegetables begin to soften and get some color. Add the cabbage and apple, stirring to incorporate; season with salt and pepper. Carefully pour the broth over the vegetables and bring up to a simmer. Reduce the heat to medium-low and simmer, uncovered, for 1 hour, until the vegetables are very tender. Add the parsley and lemon juice. Ladle the soup into soup bowls and drizzle a little olive oil on top of each serving.

POT ROAST SANDWICHES

SOME THINGS ARE EVEN BETTER THE SECOND TIME AROUND! A meal in-and-of themselves, these satisfying sandwiches take the best from the BRAISES (pages 106–135) and create something original out of intentional leftovers. While the braised meat is the jumping off point, this man-wich of a chapter is all about cross-utilizing leftovers across the board; *Citrus-Braised Cabbage*, *Pickled Red Onion*, and even *Mac 'n Cheese*, (pages 34, 4, 179), slip their way in between two slices of bread.

Since the meat is slow-roasted and tender, you want to pair it with contrasting components, like *Fried Green Tomatoes and Fresh Fig Jam* (pages 140, 146) to provide a bit of relief from the richness. These meaty sandwiches are best hot, preferably pressed in a panini grill. If you don't have one, you can achieve the same effect using a heavy skillet. At the very least, simply toast the bread to develop a textural bite and to prevent the sandwich from getting soggy.

BRAISED PORK BELLY, CARROT SLAW, CHEDDAR, SWEET-HOT MUSTARD

SERVES 4

Vietnamese baguette sandwiches, called bánh mi, have attracted a cult following in L.A. like never before. A light and chewy hoagie-style roll is stuffed with a pile of sliced salty meats, often pork, and topped with a bright, crunchy vegetable slaw. Here, rich pork belly gets a zing of flavor from shredded carrots coated with sour tamarind. To keep it SoCal, I've incorporated Cheddar cheese and sweet hot mustard to add a bit more zip.

CARROT SLAW
1 pound baby carrots, preferably assorted colors, shredded (about 2 cups)
¼ cup fresh cilantro, chopped
½ jalapeño, stemmed and thinly sliced
1 cup Tamarind Vinaigrette (see page 81)
Coarse salt and freshly ground black pepper

SANDWICH
4 bánh mi or hero rolls, halved
½ cup sweet-hot mustard, such as Beaver
1 pound Braised Pork Belly (see page 117), sliced (about 4 cups)
¼ pound sharp Cheddar cheese, sliced (about 12 slices)

TO MAKE THE CARROT SLAW, in a mixing bowl, combine the shredded carrots, cilantro, and jalapeño with the tamarind vinaigrette. Toss well to evenly coat; season with salt and pepper. Set aside at room temperature to allow the flavor to come together. You should have about 2 cups.

PREHEAT A SANDWICH PRESS according to manufacturers' instructions. If you don't have an electric press, place a grill pan or heavy skillet over medium-high heat. Brush the pan with oil.

TO BUILD THE SANDWICHES, it's important to distribute the ingredients evenly across the rolls so the sandwiches press flat. First, spread the cut sides of the rolls with 1 tablespoon of mustard. Shingle 2 slices of cheese on the bottom half of the rolls, and then divide the sliced strips of warm pork belly on top. Pile ½ cup of the slaw on the top, spreading it out to cover the surface. Put the other half of the roll on top.

PLACE THE SANDWICHES IN THE PREHEATED PANINI MAKER, grill pan, or skillet. Close the press (or, if using a grill pan, place another heavy pan on top of the sandwich to press it down). Grill until the roll is crisp on both sides, about 3 minutes. (If you're cooking the sandwich in a pan on the stove, after 3 minutes flip it over with a spatula to crisp the other side for another couple of minutes.

TO SERVE, transfer the sandwiches to a cutting board and cut diagonally in half with a sharp knife.

BBQ BRISKET, FRIED GREEN TOMATO, CHEDDAR, JALAPEÑO

SERVES 4

The added bonus about making the Traditional Beef Short Ribs (pages 109) is having leftover meat to spin into this melt-in-your-mouth panini. Fried green tomatoes and slivers of jalapeño really take this filling sandwich over the top both in richness and flavor.

4 ciabatta rolls, halved and toasted
¼ pound white Cheddar cheese, sliced (about 12 slices)
1 pound shredded BBQ Brisket (see page 110), warm (about 4 cups)
8 slices Fried Green Tomatoes (recipe follows)
1 jalapeño, stemmed and very thinly sliced

TO BUILD THE SANDWICHES, first shingle half of the cheese slices on the bottom half of the rolls, then divide the shredded meat on top. Add 2 slices of fried green tomatoes and about 4 thin slices of jalapeño to each, and finally add the remaining cheese. Put the other half of the roll on top.

TO SERVE, transfer the sandwiches to a cutting board and cut diagonally in half with a sharp knife.

FRIED GREEN TOMATOES

When shopping for green tomatoes, choose ones that are under ripe and feel very firm. If you can't locate green tomatoes, substitute red tomatoes; make sure they're not overly ripe. Serve as a side for Buttermilk-Baked Chicken (page 160) or pair with delicate baby greens and top with Green Goddess Dressing (page 83).

½ cup buttermilk
1 teaspoon Dijon mustard
1 teaspoon hot sauce, such as Tabasco
½ teaspoon paprika
½ teaspoon coarse salt
¼ teaspoon freshly ground black pepper
½ cup stone-ground cornmeal
2 large unripe green tomatoes, cut into ½-inch thick slices, ends removed (8 slices)
3 tablespoons canola oil

IN A LARGE BOWL, whisk together the buttermilk, mustard, hot sauce, paprika, salt, and pepper. Put the cornmeal in a separate bowl. Dip the tomatoes in the spicy buttermilk, then dredge in the cornmeal mixture, coating both sides well.

PLACE A LARGE CAST-IRON SKILLET over medium heat and coat with the oil. When the oil is hot, panfry the tomatoes, working in batches if necessary, until golden brown and crispy on both sides, about 3 to 4 minutes on each side. Carefully remove the tomatoes to a paper towel-lined plate.

Makes 8 slices

TRADITIONAL BEEF SHORT RIB, MAC 'N CHEESE, STEAK SAUCE

SERVES 4

This ridiculously extravagant Beef Short Rib sandwich only has four basic elements: bread, steak sauce, meat, macaroni and cheese. Toasted panini-style, the rich short rib is tender and mac and cheese adds a creamy layer of decadence. Homemade steak sauce presents a necessary amount of sweetness and tang to cut the richness. A whole meal in its self!

1 tablespoon olive oil
4 ciabatta rolls, halved
½ cup House Steak Sauce (see page 104)
½ cup Mac 'n Cheese (see page 179), warm
1 pound shredded Traditional Beef Short Rib (see page 109), warm (about 4 cups)

PREHEAT A SANDWICH PRESS according to manufacturers' instructions. If you don't have an electric press, place a grill pan or heavy skillet over medium-high heat. Brush the pan with oil.

TO BUILD THE SANDWICHES, it's important to distribute the ingredients evenly across the bread so the sandwiches press flat. First, spread the cut sides of the bread with 1 tablespoon of the steak sauce. Put ½ cup of the mac 'n cheese on the bottom half of the rolls, then divide the shredded meat on top. Put the other half of the roll on top.

PLACE THE SANDWICHES IN THE PREHEATED PANINI MAKER, grill pan, or skillet. Close the press (or, if using a pan, place another heavy pan on top of the sandwich to press it down). Grill until the ciabatta is crisp on both sides, about 3 minutes. (If you're cooking the sandwich in a pan on the stove, after 3 minutes flip it over with a spatula to crisp the other side for another couple of minutes.

TO SERVE, transfer the sandwiches to a cutting board and cut diagonally in half with a sharp knife.

RED MISO BEEF
PICKLED RED ONION, MIZUNA

SERVES 4

You don't often think of sandwiches having such a distinctive Asian flavor, but by combining shredded Red Miso Beef (page 113) with tangy Pickled Red Onion (page 3) and bitter mizuna greens, this sandwich strikes an addicting balance between French and Japanese. Miso paste helps tenderize the beef and gives the short ribs its deep, savory flavor. Serve with Forbidden Rice, Heart of Palm (page 62) and a cold Japanese beer.

1 tablespoon olive oil
4 ciabatta rolls, halved
½ cup Pickled Red Onion
  (see page 4), drained
1 pound shredded Red Miso Beef
  (see page 113), warm (about
  4 cups)
1 cup mizuna or baby mixed greens

PREHEAT A SANDWICH PRESS according to manufacturers' instructions. If you don't have an electric press, place a grill pan or heavy skillet over medium-high heat. Brush the pan with oil.

TO BUILD THE SANDWICHES, it's important to distribute the ingredients evenly across the bread so the sandwiches press flat. First put the pickled onions on the bottom half of the roll then divide the shredded meat on top. Scatter the mizuna leaves on top. Put the other half of the roll on top. Repeat with the remaining rolls.

PLACE THE SANDWICHES IN THE PREHEATED PANINI MAKER, grill pan, or skillet. Close the press (or, if using a grill pan, place another heavy pan on top of the sandwich to press it down). Grill until the ciabatta is crisp on both sides, about 3 minutes. (If you're cooking the sandwich in a pan on the stove, after 3 minutes flip it over with a spatula to crisp the other side for another couple of minutes.)

TO SERVE, transfer the sandwiches to a cutting board and cut diagonally in half with a sharp knife.

JACKSON'S PULLED PORK, CITRUS-BRAISED CABBAGE, BARBECUE SAUCE

SERVES 4

Taking a bit of my Germanic background, the satisfying pulled pork sandwich is topped with sweet-and-sour cabbage instead of traditional coleslaw. Use the tangy Citrus-Braised Cabbage, recipe (page 34) minus the goat cheese and parsley. For a taste of Southern California, swap out the rolls/hamburger buns for warm corn tortillas to make pulled pork tacos.

1 pound shredded Jackson's Pulled Pork (see page 119), warm (about 4 cups)

4 crusty white rolls or hamburger buns, halved lengthwise and toasted

2 cups Citrus-Braised Cabbage (see page 34)

PREHEAT A SANDWICH PRESS according to manufacturers' instructions. If you don't have an electric press, place a grill pan or heavy skillet over medium-high heat. Brush the pan with oil.

TO BUILD THE SANDWICHES, it's important to distribute the ingredients evenly across the bread so the sandwiches press flat. Divide the pulled pork onto the bottom half of the rolls. Pile ½ cup of the braised cabbage on the top, spreading it out to cover the surface. Put the other half of the roll on top.

PLACE THE SANDWICHES IN THE PREHEATED PANINI MAKER, grill pan, or skillet. Close the press (or, if using a grill pan, place another heavy pan on top of the sandwich to press it down). Grill until the roll is crisp on both sides, about 3 minutes. (If you're cooking the sandwich in a pan on the stove, after 3 minutes flip it over with a spatula to crisp the other side for another couple of minutes.

TO SERVE, transfer the sandwiches to a cutting board and cut diagonally in half with a sharp knife.

CHICKEN BASQUE,
MANCHEGO, FRESH FIG JAM

SERVES 4

The excellence of Basque cooking is due to the use of high-quality, local ingredients, combined with preparation that enhances, rather than masks, the natural flavor of the food. Southern California shares the same climate and culinary sensibilities with the Basque region. Remove the bones from the chicken and shred the meat of the braise before assembling the sandwich. For full effect, get a little bit of the olive and artichoke on the sandwich, too.

½ cup store-bought or **Fresh Fig Jam**
   (recipe follows)
1 tablespoon olive oil
4 ciabatta rolls, halved and toasted
¼ pound manchego cheese, sliced
1 pound Chicken Basque, Olives,
   Artichokes (see page 123), boned
   and shredded, warm (about 4 cups)

TO BUILD THE SANDWICHES, first spread the cut sides of the bread with 1 tablespoon of the fig jam. Shingle half of the cheese slices on the bottom half of the rolls, then divide the shredded chicken on top. Put the other half of the roll on top.

TO SERVE, transfer the sandwiches to a cutting board and cut diagonally in half with a sharp knife.

FRESH FIG JAM

We have the most plentiful Mission fig tree in our backyard in Sherman Oaks. During late summer, it bears so much fruit that we make enough jam to last all year. A spoonful of this rich, sweet Fresh Fig Jam is a wonderful garnish for Lamb Tagine (page 120) or include as a unique accompaniment to a cheese plate.

2 pints fresh black Mission figs,
   stemmed and coarsely chopped
½ cup sugar
½ cup water
3 tablespoons balsamic vinegar
1 teaspoon whole mustard seeds

IN A MEDIUM POT, combine the figs with the sugar, water, vinegar, and mustard seeds; bring to a simmer over medium-high heat. Stir everything together to make sure the sugar is not stuck to the bottom of the pot and the figs are well coated. Cover, and reduce the heat to medium-low. Simmer, stirring occasionally, for 45 minutes. Uncover, and continue to cook for 5 to 10 minutes until thick. Set aside to cool to room temperature.

The fig jam can easily be prepared in advance, covered, and refrigerated. It will keep for 1 month, if it lasts that long.

Makes 1 cup

LAMB TAGINE, FETA, ARUGULA

SERVES 4

The terrific bonus about making Lamb Tagine (page 120) is spinning the succulent leftovers into this melt-in-your-mouth sandwich. North Hollywood has an enclave of Middle Eastern restaurants that cook classic authentic food. A favorite among us locals is the big, juicy chunks of skewer-grilled lamb wrapped in a warm sheet of naan or fluffy pita bread. The crisp crust of ciabatta, salty feta, and bitter arugula tame the full-size flavors in the lamb. The harissa-infused mayo is good on any sandwich that can use a little spice.

½ cup mayonnaise
2 tablespoons Harissa Sauce
   (see page 89)
1 tablespoon olive oil
4 ciabatta rolls, halved
1 pound shredded Lamb Tagine
   (see page 120), warm (4 cups)
1 cup baby arugula
½ cup crumbled feta cheese

IN A SMALL BOWL, combine the mayo and harissa, mixing with a spoon until completely incorporated.

PREHEAT A SANDWICH PRESS according to manufacturers' instructions. If you don't have an electric press, place a grill pan or heavy skillet over medium-high heat. Brush the pan with oil.

TO BUILD THE SANDWICHES, it's important to distribute the ingredients evenly across the bread so the sandwiches press flat. First, spread the cut sides of the rolls with 1 tablespoon of the harissa mayonnaise. Put the feta on the bottom half of the rolls, then divide the shredded meat on top. Scatter the arugula leaves on top. Put the other half of the roll on top.

PLACE THE SANDWICHES IN THE PREHEATED PANINI MAKER, grill pan, or skillet. Close the press (or, if using a grill pan, place another heavy pan on top of the sandwich to press it down). Grill until the ciabatta is crisp on both sides and the cheese is melted, about 3 minutes. (If you're cooking the sandwich in a pan on the stove, after 3 minutes flip it over with a spatula to crisp the other side for another couple of minutes.

TO SERVE, transfer the sandwiches to a cutting board and cut diagonally in half with a sharp knife.

SEMI-TRADITIONAL SANDWICHES

THE HUMBLE SANDWICH IS A SYMBOL OF CASUAL CUISINE'S NEW SERIOUSNESS and an endless opportunity for reinvention. If you're willing to venture beyond predictable sandwiches that are just slapped together, this chapter will expand your horizons. Believe it or not, there's an art to constructing a stellar sandwich; it's all about the proportions of ingredients and how they mingle together, one should not overpower the other.

Dense, chewy bread—think sourdough or a wholesome multigrain loaf—leftover proteins from LAND + SEA (pages 86-105), crisp slaw, and moist condiments, like *Green Goddess Dressing* (page 83) create sandwiches with intriguing combinations that are unforgettable. Familiar favorites like *Egg Salad, Bacon, Heirloom Tomato* (page 166) and *Holiday Turkey, Gruyère, Cranberry Relish* (page 155) are reinvented into rustic, well thought out meals that are as satisfying as savoring a proper entree.

CHAR SIU CHICKEN, BLACK KALE, KIMCHI VEGETABLES

SERVES 4

Think of this as a healthy California wrap inspired by Chinese barbecue dim sum (bao). The irresistible little steamed buns are soft and pillowy, wrapped around a savory and sweet filling of shredded meat called Char Siu. At Lemonade, tender tortillas cradle sticky-glazed chicken, crowned with kimchi, kale, and kumquats to add an unexpected jolt of tang. These grab-and-go roll-ups make the most out of leftovers.

4 spinach tortillas, such as Mission
1 pound Char Siu Chicken (see page 94), shredded (about 4 cups)
2 cups Black Kale slaw (see page 30), or store-bought prepared kale slaw
1 cup Kimchi Vegetables (see page 44), or store-bought prepared kimchi, drained

TO BUILD THE WRAPS, lay the tortillas flat on a cutting board. Mound 1 cup of char siu chicken, ½ cup of black kale slaw, and ¼ cup of kimchi vegetables on the lower halves of the tortillas, spreading the ingredients to cover evenly. Roll up the tortilla like a burrito, tucking the sides in as you roll. Cut the wraps in half on the diagonal.

HOLIDAY TURKEY,
GRUYÈRE, CRANBERRY RELISH

SERVES 4

My father, Michael, was born and raised in England. After immigrating to the U.S., he fell in love with Thanksgiving. My formative interest in cooking stems from watching my dad skillfully carving the gigantic bird with confidence . . . even among my three American uncles. For me, the best part about Thanksgiving is transforming the leftovers into a meal equally as special.

½ cup whole grain Dijon mustard
8 slices cranberry walnut bread
   or brioche, toasted preferably
¼ pound Gruyère or Swiss, sliced
   (about 12 slices)
1 pound sliced roasted turkey breast,
   leftovers or deli
1 cup Cranberry Relish (recipe follows)
½ cup Pickled Red Onion
   (see page 4), drained

TO BUILD THE SANDWICHES, spread 1 tablespoon of mustard on each piece of toasted bread. Divide the sliced turkey evenly on 4 of the slices, which will be the bottom halves of the sandwiches. Spoon 2 tablespoons of the cranberry relish on the turkey, spreading it evenly across with the back of the spoon. Strewn 2 tablespoons of the pickled red onions all over the surface. Shingle 2 slices of the cheese on top. Put the remaining 4 slices of bread on top to enclose the sandwich. Cut the sandwiches in half on the diagonal.

CRANBERRY RELISH

The textural contrast of combining both fresh and dried cranberries gives the raw relish a pleasant, fruity chew. Superfast to prepare, this killer condiment not only pairs well with turkey, but a spoonful or two is equally awesome swirled into Greek yogurt or oatmeal for breakfast.

1 pound frozen whole cranberries,
   thawed
¼ cup dried cranberries
1 cup sugar
2 teaspoons peeled and grated
   fresh ginger
Pinch of cinnamon
Juice and finely grated zest of
   1 orange
¼ cup water

IN THE BOWL OF A FOOD PROCESSOR, combine the whole and dried cranberries, sugar, ginger, cinnamon, and orange juice and zest. Pulse to break down the cranberries and incorporate the ingredients; it should still be a bit chunky. Add the water, little by little, and pulse until the mixture reaches a chunky relish consistency.

ALLOW THE CRANBERRY RELISH TO SIT at room temperature for at least 1 hour, so the sugar dissolves and the flavors can marry. The cranberry relish can easily be prepared in advance, covered, and refrigerated.

Makes about 3 cups

CAESAR CLUB,
TURKEY, HAM, TOMATO

SERVES 4

While the most widely accepted story is that the Caesar salad was invented in Tijuana, I think of it as early California cuisine. Much more a Mediterranean fusion with California sensibilities, today the classic salad is as much L.A. as the Cobb. Here, it takes on a whole new life when shingled with tender slices of roasted meats and tomato, and swathed between crusty pieces of bread! Creamy, garlicky, and salty, this indulgent sandwich is a Lemonade classic and not to be missed. Serve poolside with a glass of Watermelon, Rosemary lemonade (page 230).

2 small hearts of Romaine, ends trimmed, dark green leaves discarded, and cut crosswise into ½-inch pieces (about 2 cups)

½ cup Caesar Dressing (see page 36)

½ cup shaved Parmesan

½ teaspoon freshly ground black pepper

½ cup mayonnaise

¼ cup whole grain Dijon mustard

8 slices whole grain bread, toasted preferably

½ pound sliced Black Forest ham

½ pound sliced roasted turkey breast, deli or leftovers

1 to 2 red Beefsteak tomatoes, cut into ¼-inch slices

IN A MIXING BOWL, combine the romaine and Caesar dressing. Toss with tongs, until the lettuce is fully and evenly coated. Sprinkle in the Parmesan and pepper, tossing again to distribute the ingredients. Set aside.

In a small bowl, combine the mayonnaise and mustard, stirring with a spoon until well blended.

TO BUILD THE SANDWICHES, spread 1 tablespoon of mayo-mustard on each piece of toasted bread. Divide the sliced ham and turkey evenly across 4 of the bread slices, which will be the bottom halves of the sandwiches. Shingle 2 slices of tomato on top. Pile ½ cup of the Caesar salad evenly across the top. Put the remaining 4 slices of bread on top to enclose the sandwich. Cut the sandwiches in half on the diagonal.

CHICKEN, BEET, APPLE, GOAT CHEESE, HONEY

SERVES 4

Embracing the fortitude of California cuisine, this Napa-style dish reconstructs the essentials of a killer cheese plate and puts them in a sandwich! Goat cheese, apple, honey, and a dose of red wine (in this case saba, see Note), kick off the base flavor, while chicken and beets provide the heft. The delectable result is an ultimate combination of meaty, earthy, and fruity. Serve with Arugula, Fig salad (page 29),

1 (4-ounce) log soft goat cheese, at room temperature

2 tablespoons saba, vin cotto, or balsamic syrup

8 slices brioche or challah bread, toasted

1 pound Greek-Marinated Chicken (see page 90), cut into ¼-inch-thick slices, at room temperature

2 cups Beet, Pickled Red Onion, Hazelnut Vinaigrette (see page 3) or store-bought prepared pickled beets, cut into cubes

½ Granny Smith apple, cored, and thickly sliced (see page 9)

4 tablespoons honey

TO BUILD THE SANDWICHES, spread 1 tablespoon of the goat cheese on each piece of toasted bread. Drizzle with 1 teaspoon of saba. Divide the chicken evenly on 4 of the bread slices, which will be the bottom halves of the sandwiches. Pile ½ cup of the beet salad on the chicken, spreading it out to cover the surface. Shingle the sliced apples on top and drizzle with honey. Put the remaining 4 slices of bread on top to enclose the sandwich. Cut the sandwiches in half on the diagonal.

SABA, VIN COTTO, BALSAMIC SYRUP

Those familiar with Italian cuisine will recognize the ingredient saba, the sweet reduction of grape must, or cooked grape juice. Saba is produced by slowly simmering the must from the trebbiano grape, the same used for balsamic vinegar, except cooked down even more, until it turns sweet and syrupy. With a wonderful fruity character, saba has notes of grape, plum, and raisin. Try drizzling it over cheesecake, dressing a fruit salad, using it in marinades, or splashing a little over ice cream. In the south of Italy, saba is called vin cotto, and in L.A. it's labeled balsamic syrup. Whatever you call it, you can find it at Italian specialty markets and well-stocked grocery stores. It's a nice item to stock in your pantry.

BUTTERMILK-BAKED CHICKEN, VIDALIA ONION-BACON CABBAGE, FRIED GREEN TOMATO, CHEDDAR

SERVES 4

At first glance, the homey ingredients of buttermilk chicken, fried green tomatoes, and Cheddar cheese may seem more Louisiana than Los Angeles, but this quintessential sandwich celebrates the car culture of the Southland in all facets. Rebellious enough to rival any great burger, Buttermilk-Baked Chicken gets the Cali treatment, sandwiched in a salty pretzel roll, slathered with herbaceous Green Goddess Dressing and spilling over with crunchy onion-bacon slaw. Serve with a Shandy. See Old-Fashioned lemonade recipe (page 225).

½ small head green cabbage
    (about ½ pound)
½ cup Vidalia Onion-Bacon
    Vinaigrette (see page 27)
½ teaspoon coarse salt
¼ teaspoon freshly ground black
    pepper
½ cup Green Goddess Dressing
    (see page 83)
4 pretzel or sourdough rolls, toasted
½ pound sliced Cheddar cheese
    (about 16 slices)
1 pound Buttermilk-Baked Chicken
    (see page 93), sliced, at room
    temperature (about 2 cups)
1 recipe Fried Green Tomatoes
    (see page 140)

CUT THE CABBAGE IN HALF AND CUT AWAY THE CORE, then thinly slice the cabbage wedges crosswise into shreds. Rinse the cabbage in a colander and allow to drain thoroughly. Put the cabbage in a mixing bowl. Pour in the onion-bacon vinaigrette and toss gently. Season with salt and pepper. You should have about 2 cups of slaw.

TO BUILD THE SANDWICHES, spread 1 tablespoon of green goddess on the top and bottom halves of the rolls. Shingle 2 slices of the cheese on the base, then divide the sliced chicken evenly on top, followed by 2 slices of fried green tomatoes. Pile ½ cup of the slaw on the top, spreading it out to cover the surface. Finally add the remaining cheese. Put the other half of the roll on top. Cut the sandwiches in half on the diagonal.

SEARED TUNA, CABBAGE GREEN APPLE SLAW, AVOCADO, SRIRACHA AIOLI, PICKLED GINGER

SERVES 4

In a city swimming with sharks, it's no wonder sushi is big in L.A. First creating a buzz here in the 1990s, Spicy Tuna Roll has now become a ubiquitous menu item in restaurants all over the country. While tuna, mayonnaise, and avocado may not be conventional Japanese, the appreciation for the quirky combo has spread nationally. At LEMONADE, those unlikely ingredients turn the tuna roll into a Japanese-inspired sandwich. Freedom and playfulness is what Southern California cooking is all about.

½ cup Sriracha Aioli (see page 100)
1 pound Seared Ahi Tuna (see page 69), sliced, at room temperature
1 cup Cabbage, Green Apple slaw (see page 32)
8 slices multigrain bread, toasted
1 firm-ripe Hass avocado, halved, pitted, peeled, and sliced
1 tablespoon pickled ginger

TO BUILD THE SANDWICHES, spread 1 tablespoon of the Sriracha aioli on each piece of toasted bread. Divide the sliced tuna evenly on 4 of the bread slices, which will be the bottom halves of the sandwiches. Pile ½ cup of the slaw on the tuna, spreading it out to cover the surface. Shingle the sliced avocado on top and strewn with the pickled ginger. Put the remaining 4 slices of bread on top to enclose the sandwich. Cut the sandwiches in half on the diagonal.

CITRUS-POACHED SALMON SALAD, SNAP PEA, CUCUMBER, GREEN GODDESS

SERVES 4

For the ladies who lunch at Lemonade, this delicate sandwich is both light and satisfying—not to mention pretty. Flaked Citrus-Poached Salmon is the base, with refreshing cucumbers, snap peas, and herbs gently folded in. Floral Green Goddess Dressing totally works as a sexy sandwich spread with a clever pun. Serve with Cucumber Mint Lemonade (page 227) or a light Rosé.

¼ pound sugar snap peas (1 cup), ends trimmed

1 Persian or kirby cucumber, halved lengthwise, seeds scooped out with a spoon, and diced

1 tablespoon fresh dill, chopped

1 tablespoon fresh tarragon leaves, chopped

½ cup Champagne Vinaigrette (see page 11)

Juice of ½ lemon

1 pound Citrus-Poached Salmon (see page 99), chilled and flaked (about 2 cups)

½ teaspoon coarse salt

¼ teaspoon freshly ground black pepper

½ cup Green Goddess Dressing (see page 83)

8 slices brioche or challah bread, toasted

4 whole butter lettuce leaves

BRING A LARGE POT OF WELL SALTED WATER TO A BOIL OVER HIGH HEAT. Prepare an ice bath by filling a large bowl halfway with water and adding a tray of ice cubes.

BLANCH THE SNAP PEAS FOR ONLY ABOUT 2 MINUTES; they become tender very quickly. Using a slotted spoon, remove the snap peas from the water and plunge into the ice bath to "shock" them, i.e., to stop the cooking process and cool them down right away. This procedure also sets the vibrant green color of the peas. Drain the snap peas in a colander.

THINLY SLICE THE BLANCHED SNAP PEAS on the diagonal and place into a mixing bowl. Add the cucumbers, dill, and tarragon. Toss with the Champagne vinaigrette and lemon juice to evenly coat. Add the salmon and gently toss again to distribute. Season with salt and pepper. You should have about 4 cups of the salad.

TO BUILD THE SANDWICHES, spread 1 tablespoon of the green goddess dressing on each piece of toasted bread. Divide the salmon salad evenly on 4 of the bread slices, which will be the bottom halves of the sandwiches. Lay a piece of lettuce on top. Put the remaining 4 slices of bread on top to enclose the sandwiches. Cut the sandwiches in half on the diagonal.

EGG SALAD, BACON, HEIRLOOM TOMATO

SERVES 4

There's a slew of great Jewish delis in L.A., Langer's downtown being a longstanding favorite. While egg salad may not sound all that exciting, their rendition has the essence of fine caviar. Instead of just mashing boiled eggs together, they take the extra step to whip the yolks into a yellow mousse and then fold in the hand-chopped whites separately. This simple method makes all of the difference in creating interesting texture and flavor. At Lemonade, we take the inspiration to the next level by adding pungent flavors like pickle juice, hot sauce, chives, and mustard. Topped with slices of crispy bacon and ripe tomato, this sandwich makes the most out of everyday ingredients.

8 large eggs

½ cup mayonnaise, plus more for smearing on sandwich

1 generous tablespoon yellow mustard

1½ teaspoons pickle juice or lemon juice

2 dashes of hot sauce, such as Tabasco

2 tablespoons finely chopped fresh chives

½ shallot, finely chopped

½ teaspoon coarse salt

½ teaspoon freshly ground black pepper

8 slices whole grain bread, toasted

1 to 2 heirloom tomatoes, sliced

8 strips smoked bacon, cooked

PUT THE EGGS IN A LARGE, WIDE POT, cover with 1 inch of cool water over medium-high heat. Starting with cold water and gently bringing the eggs to a boil will help keep them from cracking. Once the water boils, turn off the heat, cover the pot, and let the eggs sit in the hot water for 15 minutes.

IN THE MEANTIME, PREPARE AN ICE BATH by filling a large bowl halfway with water and adding a tray of ice cubes. The key here is to cool the eggs quickly. Why? It's the best way to prevent discoloration around the yolk and makes them easy to peel.

USING A STRAINER OR SLOTTED SPOON, remove the eggs to the ice bath. Allow them to sit in the water for 5 minutes so they are completely cool down to the center.

ONE AT A TIME, GIVE EACH EGG a few gentle taps on the kitchen counter; you want to crack the shell while trying not to damage the white underneath. Gently, roll the egg around until the shell has small cracks all over it and peel it off.

USING A PARING KNIFE, HALVE THE EGGS lengthwise and pop the yolks out and into a food processor. Add the mayonnaise, mustard, pickle juice, and hot sauce; season with salt and pepper. Puree until completely smooth. Transfer to a mixing bowl. Coarsely chop the whites, add them to the bowl, and gently fold so they are well coated in the yolk puree. Fold in the chives and shallot.

TO BUILD THE SANDWICHES, divide the egg salad on 4 of the bread slices, which will be the bottom halves of the sandwiches. Shingle 2 slices of tomato and 2 strips of bacon on top of the egg salad. Spread a little mayonnaise on the remaining 4 slices of bread and put on top to enclose the sandwich.

SOUPS +
STUFF

THIS SMALL BUT MIGHTY CHAPTER features a collection of Lemonade's most popular side dishes. Fresh vegetable soups like *Corn Chowder* (page 171) and *Creamed Cauliflower Soup* (page 172) provide the majority of the recipes. Making soup teaches you how to think about the compatibility of ingredients, the roles of assembly and cooking times, and the balance of flavors. Once you've learned to make soup, you'll feel confident in tackling anything. Full-bodied, yet not heavy-handed, *Chicken Chili* (page 178) and *Mac 'n Cheese* (page 179) make a fine accompaniment to any of the sandwiches or can be your entire meal!

CORN CHOWDER

MAKES 8 CUPS

Fresh, sweet corn, especially in the summer when it's in season, has a pure taste, with kernels almost bursting off of the cob. Corn takes center stage in this soothing, light soup with potatoes adding a creamy body and cayenne just a little kick. This Corn Chowder is terrific warm or chilled. For a hearty variation, replace 1 cup of the broth with clam juice and add 2 cans of chopped clams for an entire Malibu clambake in a bowl!

2 tablespoons canola oil

1 large onion, diced

2 celery stalks, halved lengthwise
   and chopped

2 garlic cloves, chopped

1 teaspoon coarse salt

½ teaspoon freshly ground black
   pepper

1 teaspoon chopped fresh thyme
   leaves

½ teaspoon cayenne pepper

2 tablespoons all-purpose flour

1½ quarts vegetable broth

1 Idaho potato, peeled and diced

5 ears fresh corn, shucked, kernels
   cut from cob (about 4 cups)

2 cups half-and-half

Chopped fresh flat-leaf parsley or
   scallions, for garnish

COAT A SOUP POT WITH THE OIL and put over medium heat. When the oil is hot, add the onion, celery, and garlic. Cook and stir until the vegetables begin to soften but do not brown, about 10 minutes. Season with salt and pepper. Stir in the thyme, cayenne, and flour. Cook and stir for about 2 minutes to incorporate the flour, taking care to break up any clumps.

POUR IN THE BROTH, increase the heat to medium-high, and bring to boil. Add the potatoes and simmer until fork tender, about 15 minutes, stirring occasionally.

Reduce the heat to medium-low, add the corn and half-and-half. Gently simmer until the soup is thickened slightly, about 5 minutes. Garnish with chopped parsley and/or scallions.

CREAMED CAULIFLOWER SOUP

MAKES 8 CUPS

In L.A., where cocktail dresses pass for daywear and executives wear flip-flops to board meetings, this soup follows suit dressed up with a dollop of caviar or modestly sipped from a coffee cup. Down-to-earth and stylish at the same time, cauliflower and potato are pureed into a smooth, winter-white soup. Thickened with potatoes and just a bit of cream, the mouth-feel is silky without tasting too rich. Creamed Cauliflower Soup doubles as a luxurious sauce pooled under seared scallops. Serve with Smoked Salmon, Watercress Salad (page 73) or crusty French bread.

2 tablespoons canola oil

1 onion, halved and sliced

3 garlic cloves, smashed

1 head cauliflower (about 2 pounds), coarsely chopped, including stems

2 bay leaves, preferably fresh

1 teaspoon coarse salt, plus more for serving

½ teaspoon freshly ground black pepper, plus more for serving

1½ quarts low-sodium chicken broth

2 Idaho potatoes, peeled and diced

1 cup heavy cream

COAT A SOUP POT WITH THE OIL AND PLACE OVER MEDIUM HEAT. When the oil is hot, add the onion, garlic, cauliflower, and bay leaves. Cook and stir until the vegetables begin to soften but do not brown, about 5 minutes. Season with salt and pepper.

POUR IN THE BROTH, increase the heat to medium-high, and bring to a boil. Simmer for 15 minutes, stirring occasionally. Add the potatoes and continue to cook until fork tender, 10 to 15 minutes.

REDUCE THE HEAT TO MEDIUM-LOW, pour in the cream, and gently simmer until thickened slightly, about 5 minutes.

WORKING IN BATCHES, ladle the soup into a blender filling it no more than halfway. Puree for a few seconds until completely smooth; be sure to hold down the lid with a kitchen towel for safety. If you have an immersion blender, this is a great time to use it.

IF DESIRED, PASS THE SOUP THROUGH a fine-mesh strainer into a terrine or other pot, pushing the solids with the back of a wooden spoon. Discard the vegetable pieces. Repeat with the remaining soup. Divide among soup bowls or coffee cups. Season each serving with a pinch of salt and pepper.

TORTILLA SOUP

MAKES 8 CUPS

The origin of Tortilla Soup may be south of the border, but the intriguing flavor has long made it a California favorite. Between the smoky spices, soothing tomato broth, and pile of fixings, what's not to love? While there are many variations, it's the ground tortillas that give the soup a unique thickness and flavor. Simple to prepare, skip straining this blended soup for a more rustic presentation. If you want to add protein, top with shredded chicken or black beans.

2 tablespoons canola oil
1 large onion, chopped
4 garlic cloves, minced
1 teaspoon coarse salt
1 teaspoon chili powder
½ teaspoon cayenne pepper
½ teaspoon ground cumin
1 tablespoon fresh oregano leaves, chopped
1 (28-ounce) can diced tomatoes, with juice
1½ quarts low-sodium chicken broth
3 cups fried corn tortilla strips, plus more for serving
Cubed avocado, cilantro, sour cream, shredded cheese, and lime wedges, for serving

COAT A SOUP POT WITH THE OIL and put over medium heat. When the oil is hot, add the onion and garlic. Cook and stir until the onion begins to soften but not brown, about 3 minutes. Season with salt, chili powder, cayenne, cumin, and oregano. Cook and stir for about 2 minutes or until the spices become fragrant, taking care not to burn. Pour in the diced tomatoes and broth. Simmer until the tomatoes thicken slightly, about 15 minutes, stirring occasionally.

INCREASE THE HEAT TO MEDIUM-HIGH, and bring the soup to a boil. Add the tortilla chips. Simmer until the chips soften and break down into the soup, about 15 minutes, stirring occasionally.

WORKING IN BATCHES, ladle the soup into a blender filling it no more than halfway. Puree for a few seconds until completely smooth; be sure to hold down the lid with a kitchen towel for safety. If you have an immersion blender, this is a great time to use it.

IF DESIRED, PASS THE SOUP THROUGH a fine-mesh strainer into a terrine or other pot, pushing the solids with the back of a wooden spoon. Discard the vegetable pieces. Repeat with the remaining soup. Season with a pinch of salt and pepper if needed.

SERVE THE SOUP WITH YOUR FAVORITE TOPPINGS, such as tortilla chips, avocado, cilantro, sour cream, shredded cheese, and fresh lime.

FENNEL, FARRO SOUP

MAKES 8 CUPS

Wild fennel grows up and down the hillsides and canyons of L.A. In fact, it's almost everywhere in Southern California. It's found up and down the state, from San Diego to Silicon Valley. Though it seems to have adopted California as a second home, fennel is a staple in Tuscany, which shares our same hot, dry weather. When you're feeling a little run down or craving something light, this clean-tasting soup fits the bill. The mellow anise flavor of the fennel and chewy nuttiness of the farro make this straightforward soup a standout. To bulk up into a main meal, add diced Greek-Marinated Chicken (page 90) or white beans. Equally as enjoyable warm as it is at room temperature, this soup goes from good to great when dressed with extra-virgin olive oil and grated Parmesan cheese.

1 leek, white and pale green part only
1 tablespoon olive oil
1 fennel bulb, halved, cored, and thinly sliced crosswise, and fennel fronds chopped and reserved
2 celery stalks, trimmed, halved lengthwise and chopped
2 garlic cloves, minced
2 quarts vegetable broth
½ cup farro
Juice of 1 lemon
½ teaspoon coarse salt
¼ teaspoon freshly ground black pepper
Extra-virgin olive oil and grated Parmesan cheese, for serving

HALVE THE LEEKS LENGTHWISE and then cut crosswise into ½-inch pieces. Put the sliced leeks in a colander and rinse really well under cool water, checking for dirt between the layers. Drain well; you should have about 2 cups of sliced leeks.

COAT A SOUP POT with the oil and put over medium heat. When the oil is hot, add the leek, fennel bulb, and celery. Cook, stirring, until the vegetables are tender, about 10 minutes. Add the garlic and cook for 2 minutes.

POUR IN THE BROTH, increase the heat to medium-high, and bring to boil. Add the farro, cover, and simmer until the fennel and farro are tender, about 15 minutes, stirring occasionally.

ADD THE FENNEL FRONDS AND LEMON JUICE. Season with salt and pepper. Serve the soup with a drizzle of olive oil and freshly grated Parmesan cheese.

CHICKEN CHILI

MAKES 10 CUPS

A lighter alternative to beef, this easy Chicken Chili is just right for a stress-free weeknight dinner or tailgate party; it comes together in just over an hour yet tastes as if it's been simmering on the stovetop all day. The smokiness of the chili is really satisfying, without being heavy or overly spicy. Add a can of kidney beans for extra nutrition. It's important that the vegetables in the base are cut small, so they have a consistent texture with the ground chicken and melt into the chili. You can do this easily in a food processor. Serve with Green Tomato, Sweet Corn (page 12).

¼ cup vegetable oil
2 large onions, finely chopped
3 carrots, finely chopped
3 celery stalks, finely chopped
3 pounds ground chicken, both white and dark meat
2 tablespoons ground cumin
2 tablespoons ground chili powder
2 tablespoons smoked paprika
2 tablespoons granulated onion
2 tablespoons dried sage
1 tablespoon coarse salt
1½ teaspoons freshly ground black pepper
2 tablespoons all-purpose flour
1 (28-ounce) can crushed tomatoes
1 quart low-sodium chicken broth

PUT A LARGE DUTCH OVEN or pot over medium-high heat and coat with the oil. When the oil is hot, add the onions, carrot, and celery. Cook, stirring, until the vegetables begin to soften and brown, about 10 minutes.

ADD THE GROUND CHICKEN TO THE POT, breaking it up with the back of a wooden spoon. Cook until the chicken is no longer pink, about 5 minutes.

SPRINKLE IN THE CUMIN, chili powder, paprika, granulated onion, sage, salt, and pepper. Cook and stir to incorporate the spices, about 2 minutes. Sprinkle in the flour, stirring constantly, to incorporate and cook out the raw taste.

POUR IN THE CAN OF TOMATOES, along with their liquid, and the broth. Reduce the heat to medium-low. Gently simmer, uncovered, until the chili is thick, about 1 hour, stirring occasionally.

MAC 'N CHEESE

SERVES 6 TO 8

Everyone should know how to make macaroni and cheese; the gooey cheesy goodness makes even a bad day better. This universally loved dish can be found on upscale menus redolent of truffle oil or baked country-style topped with buttery breadcrumbs. At Lemonade, we incorporate strong-flavored cheeses like blue and Parmesan to impart a grown-up taste to a childhood favorite. Serve with Buttermilk-Baked Chicken (page 93) or as a sandwich component with Traditional Beef Short Rib (page 109).

1 pound elbow macaroni
4 tablespoons unsalted butter
4 tablespoons all-purpose flour
1 quart milk
4 cups shredded sharp Cheddar cheese
½ cup crumbled blue cheese
1 cup grated Parmesan cheese
½ teaspoon coarse salt
½ teaspoon freshly ground black pepper
½ teaspoon paprika

PREHEAT THE OVEN TO 350 DEGREES F.

BRING A LARGE POT OF SALTED WATER TO A BOIL, add the macaroni, and cook for about 10 minutes, until tender but still firm. Drain well and set aside.

IN A DEEP SKILLET OR POT, melt the butter over medium heat. Sprinkle in the flour to make a roux and cook, stirring constantly, to break up any lumps. Once the roux is smooth, pour in the milk and cook until the mixture is thick, still stirring all the while. Stir in 3 cups of the Cheddar a handful at a time, and continue to cook and stir until the cheese melts. Stir in the blue and Parmesan cheeses; season with salt, pepper, and paprika.

ADD THE COOKED MACARONI AND FOLD TO INCORPORATE. Transfer the macaroni mixture to a 13-x-9-inch baking dish. Sprinkle the top with the remaining cup of shredded Cheddar cheese. Bake for 30 minutes, until hot and bubbly.

SWEDISH KNÄCKEBRÖD (CRISPBREAD)

MAKES 1 DOZEN

Eaten year round in Sweden, these thin, extra-large crackers became trendy in L.A. as a lighter alternative to bread. Oats make the wafers extra-crunchy with a crisp wholesome texture, perfectly delicious with soup or salads, or with a smear of Fresh Fig Jam (page 146). Play around with types of flour; whole wheat and rye produces a cracker with denser texture.

2⅓ cups all-purpose flour, plus more for dusting
1⅓ cups rolled oats
3 tablespoons sugar
½ teaspoon baking soda
½ teaspoon salt
½ cup grated Parmesan cheese
½ cup (1 stick) unsalted butter, cold and cut into chunks
⅓ cup vegetable shortening
½ cup buttermilk

IN A MIXING BOWL, combine the dry ingredients; the flour, oats, sugar, baking powder, salt, and ¼ cup of the Parmesan. Using a fork or a pastry blender, cut in the butter and shortening to coat the dry ingredients, the mixture should look like coarse crumbs. Pour in the buttermilk and fold together just to incorporate; be sure not to overmix the dough, it will be wet. Wrap the dough in plastic wrap and refrigerate for at least 30 minutes to firm up.

PREHEAT THE OVEN TO 325 DEGREES F. Line 2 baking pans with wax paper or parchment.

REMOVE THE DOUGH FROM THE REFRIGERATOR and set it out on the counter for 5 minutes to warm up a bit, making it easier to roll out. Sprinkle the counter and a rolling pin lightly with flour. Roll the dough out thinly, about ⅛ inch thick.

CUT THE DOUGH INTO LARGE RECTANGLES, about the size of an iPhone. Carefully transfer the rectangles to the prepared pans. Sprinkle the tops with the remaining ¼ cup of Parmesan. Bake for 12 to 15 minutes, until the crackers begin to crisp around the edges and are firm to the touch.

SWEETS

red velvet cake

IT WOULDN'T BE L.A. WITHOUT THE SUGAR ON TOP! Eating healthy sprinkled with a bit of sweet indulgence is the city's idea of balance! No matter what health craze may swoop the nation next, sweets will always remain the perfect ending.

While dessert connotes an aura of the forbidden, a decadent way to spoil ourselves, the act of baking signifies nurturing. When it comes to dessert, people gravitate to something homey, comfortable, and familiar; those they can relate to and fondly remember. Nostalgic desserts like *Oatmeal Golden Raisin Cookies*, *Carrot Cupcakes*, and *Pineapple Upside-Down Cake* (page 189, 198, 216), don't necessarily reinvent the wheel, but despite better judgment, you can't help but finish.

Whether it's a birthday cake, weekend brunch, or sweets for a bake sale, this chapter is full of pleasing and familiar dishes, something memorably reminiscent of other treats that you can't quite put your finger on.

Dessert is an important part of any meal; it's the last thing people remember eating and the sensation is something that compels us to linger a little longer at the table. Suitable for a backyard barbecue, holiday feast, or a casual dinner party with friends, these recipes truly offer inspiration. You don't have to be a pastry chef to master these delicious desserts, you just need a sweet tooth and a passion for warm, deep flavors that are timeless.

PEANUT BUTTER-
MILK CHOCOLATE COOKIES

MAKES 1 DOZEN

There are those people on the planet that love any and all things peanut butter, my mother, Alana, being one of them. Whenever she comes into Lemonade, they warm these Peanut Butter–Milk Chocolate Cookies up for my mom. Simultaneously satisfying the craving for peanut butter and chocolate, these cookies are not too sweet and not too overwhelmingly peanut buttery. When the cookies come out of the oven the smell is intoxicating.

¾ cup all-purpose flour
1 teaspoon baking soda
½ teaspoon salt
½ cup (1 stick) unsalted butter, at room temperature
½ cup light brown sugar, loosely packed
½ cup granulated sugar
½ cup creamy peanut butter
1 large egg
1 teaspoon natural vanilla extract
½ cup milk chocolate chips

PREHEAT THE OVEN TO 350 DEGREES F. Grease two baking pans or line with wax or parchment paper; set aside.

IN A MIXING BOWL, combine the flour, baking soda, and salt; set aside. Put the butter and sugars in the bowl of a standing electric mixer fitted with a paddle attachment, or use a hand-held electric beater. Beat on medium speed until light and fluffy, about 3 minutes. Scrape down the sides of the bowl. Add the peanut butter, beating well to incorporate. Add the egg and continue to beat until well combined.

TURN THE MIXER TO LOW SPEED and slowly add the dry ingredients to the creamed butter and sugar mixture in 2 additions, beating just to combine. Do not overmix or the cookie dough can become tough. Turn the mixer off and fold in the chocolate chips with a rubber spatula, until evenly distributed.

USING YOUR PALMS, roll the dough into 2-inch balls, about the size of a golf ball. Alternatively, you can use a small ice cream scoop. Put the dough on the prepared pans, about 2-inches apart. Bake for 12 to 15 minutes, until the cookies are just set on the edges but still fairly soft in the center. Cool in the pans for 5 minutes, then transfer to a wire rack to cool completely.

CLASSIC CHOCOLATE CHIP COOKIES

MAKES 1 DOZEN

Chocolate Chip Cookies have become an American icon, right up there with apple pie and Red Velvet Cake (page 212). Crisp at the edges, soft in the middle, this foolproof recipe pretty much sums up what everyone is looking for in their chocolate chip cookie nirvana. Err on the side of under-baking to ensure the cookies come out moist. For a crowd-pleasing assortment of textures and flavors, put together a cookie plate, including Peanut Butter–Milk Chocolate Cookies (page 185) and Oatmeal Golden Raisin Cookies (page 189).

1⅓ cups all-purpose flour
½ teaspoon baking soda
1 teaspoon salt
½ cup (1 stick) unsalted butter, at room temperature
½ cup light brown sugar, loosely packed
1 large egg
½ teaspoon natural vanilla extract
1¼ cups semisweet chocolate chips

PREHEAT THE OVEN TO 350 DEGREES F. Grease two baking pans or line with wax or parchment paper; set aside.

IN A MIXING BOWL, combine the flour, baking soda, and salt; set aside. Put the butter and sugar in the bowl of a standing electric mixer fitted with a paddle attachment, or use a handheld electric beater. Beat on medium speed until light and fluffy, about 3 minutes. Scrape down the sides of the bowl. Add the egg and vanilla, beating well to incorporate.

TURN THE MIXER TO LOW SPEED and slowly add the dry ingredients to the creamed butter and sugar mixture in 2 additions, beating just to combine. Do not over-mix or the cookie dough can become tough. Turn the mixer off and fold in the chocolate chips with a rubber spatula until evenly distributed.

USING YOUR PALMS, roll the dough into 2-inch balls, about the size of a golf ball. Alternatively, you can use a small ice cream scoop. Put the dough on the prepared baking pans, about 2-inches apart. Bake for 15 to 20 minutes, until the cookies are just set on the edges but still fairly soft in the center. Cool in the pans for 5 minutes, then transfer to a wire rack to cool completely.

OATMEAL GOLDEN RAISIN COOKIES

MAKES 1 DOZEN

It's your mom's oatmeal cookie, just way better. More like a granola bar than a dense, chewy cookie, these Oatmeal Golden Raisin Cookies are packed with heaps of oats, plenty of raisins, and molasses to bring out a deeper flavor. The cookies spread out quite a bit while baking, making them relatively flat and the edges crispy. Orange zest and cinnamon balances the sweetness. Try not to eat them for breakfast!

¾ cup all-purpose flour
¼ teaspoon baking soda
¼ teaspoon salt
½ teaspoon ground cinnamon or nutmeg
¼ cup (½ stick) unsalted butter, at room temperature
½ cup sugar
1 large egg
1 tablespoon light corn syrup
2 teaspoons molasses
½ teaspoon natural vanilla extract
½ teaspoon finely grated orange zest
1 cup rolled oats
½ cup golden raisins

PREHEAT THE OVEN TO 350 DEGREES F. Grease two baking pans or line with wax or parchment paper; set aside.

IN A MIXING BOWL, combine the flour, baking soda, salt, and cinnamon or nutmeg; set aside. Put the butter and sugar in the bowl of a standing electric mixer fitted with a paddle attachment, or use a handheld electric beater. Beat on medium speed until light and fluffy, about 3 minutes. Scrape down the sides of the bowl. Add the egg, corn syrup, molasses, vanilla, and zest, beating well to incorporate.

TURN THE MIXER TO LOW SPEED and slowly add the dry ingredients to the creamed butter and sugar mixture in 2 additions, beating just to combine. Do not overmix or the cookie dough can become tough. Turn the mixer off and fold in the oats and raisins using a rubber spatula until evenly distributed.

USING YOUR PALMS, roll the dough into 2-inch balls, about the size of a golf ball. Alternatively, you can use a small ice cream scoop. Put the dough on the prepared pans, about 2-inches apart. Bake for 12 to 15 minutes, until the cookies are just set on the edges but still fairly soft in the center. Cool in the pans for 5 minutes, then transfer to a wire rack to cool completely.

RASPBERRY LINZER
TART COOKIES

MAKES 1 DOZEN

Essentially the baking equivalent of fresh snow, Linzer Tart Cookies is a traditional treat at holiday time. Typically filled with raspberry jam, these sandwich cookies feature a decorative cutout in the top of the cookie so the fruit filling peeks through. As odd as it sounds, hard-boiled egg yolks mixed into the dough is key, producing cookies with a unique melt-in-your-mouth texture and delicate crumb.

1 cup (2 sticks) butter, cut into cubes
¾ cup granulated sugar
4 large hard-boiled egg yolks,
    pressed through a fine-mesh sieve
1 tablespoon dark rum or rum extract
2 teaspoons ground cinnamon
¼ teaspoon salt
½ cup fine-grain almond meal or flour
2½ cups all-purpose flour, plus more
    for dusting
2 teaspoons baking powder
1 (8-ounce) jar seedless raspberry jam
½ cup powdered sugar, for dusting

PUT THE BUTTER AND GRANULATED SUGAR in the bowl of a standing electric mixer fitted with a paddle attachment, or use a hand-held electric beater. Beat on medium speed until light and fluffy, about 3 minutes. Scrape down the sides of the bowl. Add the egg yolks, rum, cinnamon, and salt. Gradually sprinkle in the almond meal, beating well to combine. Add the flour and baking powder, beating just until incorporated. Divide the dough in half, form into disks, wrap in plastic and refrigerate for at least 30 minutes or up to 2 days to firm up.

PREHEAT THE OVEN TO 350 DEGREES F. Grease two baking pans or line with wax or parchment paper; set aside.

REMOVE THE DOUGH FROM THE REFRIGERATOR and set it out on the counter for 5 minutes to warm up a bit, making it easier to roll out. Sprinkle the counter and a rolling pin lightly with flour. Working with one disc at a time, roll the dough out thinly, about ⅛-inch-thick.

USING A 3-INCH ROUND COOKIE CUTTER with scalloped edges, stamp out as many rounds as possible. Gather the dough scraps and reroll, cutting out the rest of the cookies; you should end up with 24 rounds. For the top of the cookies, take 12 of the cookies, and using a small cookie cutter, punch out a small circle (diamond, heart, or other shape you have) in the center, so it looks like a donut.

USING A SMALL SPATULA, arrange the bottom halves of the cookies on the prepared pans. Dip your finger in water and rub it around the outside of the circle. Place the cutout circles on top, gently pressing down to glue the cookie sandwiches together. Bake 10 to 12 minutes, until they're lightly browned on the edges. Transfer the cookies to a wire cooling rack to completely cool.

SPOON THE RASPBERRY JAM INTO THE HOLES in the centers then lightly dust powdered sugar all over the tops the cookies. Let stand for several hours, until the filling is set.

ALMOND MEAL

Also labeled almond flour, almond meal can be found in most markets. The finer the grain, the smoother the cookie surface will be. You can also pulse blanched almonds to a fine consistency.

CARAMEL FLEUR DE SEL
MACARONS

MAKES 1 DOZEN

In Los Angeles, brightly colored French macarons are labeled as "the new cupcake"; pastry shops everywhere carry them and they're now even showing up in grocery stores. While delicious if made well, those adorable two-bite little domes of almond meringue are a bit too precious to finish off a meal at Lemonade. Going against trend, these giant flying saucers of chewy sandwich cookies are more moon pie than minuscule macaron.

COOKIES
1½ cups fine-grain almond meal
  or flour (see page 191)
2 cups powdered sugar
½ teaspoon ground cinnamon
3 large egg whites, at room
  temperature
2 tablespoons granulated sugar
1 tablespoon Fleur de Sel, for
  sprinkling

FILLING
1 (8-ounce) package cream cheese,
  at room temperature
½ cup powdered sugar
3 tablespoons Caramel, cooled
  (recipe follows)

LINE TWO BAKING PANS WITH WAX OR PARCHMENT PAPER and have a pastry bag fitted with a plain tip ready (see page 000); set aside.

TO PREPARE THE BATTER, in a blender or food processor, grind together the almond meal, powdered sugar, and cinnamon so there are no lumps. Sift through a fine-mesh sieve into a bowl.

PUT THE EGG WHITES IN THE BOWL of a standing electric mixer fitted with a whisk attachment, or use a handheld electric beater. Beat on medium speed until foamy. While whipping, gradually sprinkle in the granulated sugar. Continue to whip until the whites become thick, glossy, and stiff peaks form about 3 minutes.

USING A RUBBER SPATULA, carefully fold the dry ingredients into the beaten egg whites, working in two batches. Be quick but gentle, and be sure to scrape down any flour that sticks to the sides of bowl. When the mixture is just smooth and there are no streaks of egg white, stop folding and scrape the batter into the pastry bag.

PIPE THE BATTER ON THE PREPARED PANS into 2-inch circles, evenly spaced apart. You should have 12 per pan. Tap the pans a few times firmly on the counter top to level and knock out any air bubbles. Set aside at room temperature for at least 1 hour to form a dry skin on the surface; this creates the cookie's distinctive crisp shell.

PREHEAT THE OVEN TO 325 DEGREES F.

SPRINKLE THE TOPS WITH THE FLEUR DE SEL. Bake the macarons for 15 to 18 minutes until the cookies are pale golden. Let cool completely in the pans before filling and sandwiching.

TO PREPARE THE FILLING, put the cream cheese in the bowl of a standing electric mixer fitted with a paddle attachment, or use a handheld electric beater. Beat on medium speed until very smooth and lump-free, about 2 minutes. Stop the machine periodically to scrape the cream cheese off the paddle and the sides of the bowl. While beating, gradually sprinkle in the powdered sugar until light and fluffy, about 3 minutes. Add the caramel and continue to mix until completely combined.

TO ASSEMBLE, using a spoon or small spatula, spread a bit of the caramel filling on the tops of the macarons then sandwich them together. Store in an airtight container for up to 5 days, or freeze.

PASTRY BAG

If you don't have a pastry bag, no worries a plastic storage bag does the trick. Take a large resealable plastic storage bag and turn it inside out. Using a spatula, scoop the frosting into the corner of the bag. Then turn bag right side out, and push the frosting all the way down into the corner of the bag. Snip the corner of the bag off with sharp scissors and you're ready to begin piping.

CARAMEL

Caramel is essentially melted sugar transformed into a thick golden liquid. Making caramel can be sticky business; it goes from glistening to a burnt mess in the blink of eye, but when you nail it, the outcome is extraordinary. Perfect caramel should smell nutty and be cooked until it looks dark, reddish-brown, like an old copper penny. You must keep watch on it though, because once burnt, caramel can't be saved. A spritz of lemon juice helps keep the caramel smooth. Extremely versatile, make a double batch and use the caramel as a dip for fresh apple slices or to top Butterscotch Pudding (page 217).

¼ cup water
1 cup granulated sugar
Juice of ½ lemon
¼ cup (½ stick) unsalted butter,
   cut into chunks
½ cup heavy cream

PREPARE THE CARAMEL, combine the water, sugar, and lemon juice in a pot over medium-high heat; it should look like wet sand. Cook until the sugar melts and begins to turn golden, about 5 minutes. Continue to cook, swirling the pot over the burner, until the color deepens to medium amber, about 3 minutes more. Be careful, the sugar is really hot at this point. Stir in the butter, which will foam a little bit, and continue to cook just to combine, about 1 minute.

REDUCE THE HEAT TO LOW AND POUR IN THE CREAM; be careful because it will sputter a bit. When the bubbling has subsided, stir the caramel, and pour into a heatproof container to cool to room temperature.

Makes 1 cup

PISTACHIO MACARONS

MAKES 1 DOZEN

The central coast of California, near Paso Robles, may be best known for its wines, but the region is also the second largest pistachio grower in the world. Instead of using all almond flour in the batter, the addition of ground pistachios adds an extra chewiness and intense nutty flavor. The basic meringue-style French macaron is merely the springboard for your wildest color and flavor combinations. Here, green food coloring signals the tantalizingly crisp cookies are primed with pistachio.

COOKIES

½ cup fine-grain almond meal or flour (see page 191)

1 cup shelled pistachios

2 cups powdered sugar

3 large egg whites, at room temperature

2 tablespoons granulated sugar

1 teaspoon green food coloring

FILLING

1 (8-ounce) package cream cheese, at room temperature

½ cup powdered sugar

LINE TWO BAKING SHEETS with wax or parchment paper and have a pastry bag fitted with a plain tip ready (see page 000); set aside.

TO PREPARE THE BATTER, in a blender or food processor, grind together the almond meal, pistachios, and powdered sugar so there are no lumps. Sift through a fine-mesh sieve into a bowl.

PUT THE EGG WHITES IN THE BOWL of a standing electric mixer fitted with a whisk attachment, or use a hand-held electric beater. Beat on medium speed until foamy. While whipping, gradually sprinkle in the granulated sugar. Add the food coloring. Continue to whip until the whites become green, thick, glossy, and stiff peaks form, about 3 minutes.

USING A RUBBER SPATULA, carefully fold the dry ingredients into the beaten egg whites, working in two batches. Be quick but gentle, and be sure to scrape down any flour that sticks to the sides of bowl. When the mixture is just smooth and there are no streaks of egg white, stop folding and scrape the batter into the pastry bag.

PIPE THE BATTER ON THE PREPARED PANS into 2-inch circles, evenly spaced apart. You should have 12 per pan. Tap the pans a few times firmly on the counter top to level and knock out any air bubbles. Set aside at room temperature for at least 1 hour to form a dry skin on the surface; this creates the cookie's distinctive crisp shell.

PREHEAT THE OVEN TO 325 DEGREES F. Bake the macarons for 15 to 18 minutes until the cookies are pale golden. Let cool completely in the pans before filling and sandwiching.

TO PREPARE THE FILLING, put the cream cheese in the bowl of a standing electric mixer fitted with a paddle attachment, or use a hand-held electric beater. Beat on medium speed until very smooth and lump-free, about 2 minutes. Stop the machine periodically to scrape the cream cheese off the paddle and the sides of the bowl. While beating, gradually sprinkle in the powdered sugar until light and fluffy, about 3 minutes.

TO ASSEMBLE, using a spoon or small spatula, spread a bit of the filling on the tops of the macarons then sandwich them together. Store in an airtight container for up to 5 days, or freeze.

LEMON DROP CUPCAKES

MAKES 1 DOZEN STANDARD-SIZE CUPCAKES OR 16 MINI CUPCAKES

Nothing says sunshine in the kitchen like lemon. These Lemon Drop Cupcakes not only look spectacular but also get a double dose of Vitamin C in both the cake and the tart lemon topping. Moist, zingy, and beautifully garnished with a kiss of lemon curd, if you're a lemon lover, this is the dessert to try.

BATTER
1½ cups all-purpose flour
1½ teaspoons baking powder
¼ teaspoon salt
½ cup (1 stick) unsalted butter
1 cup sugar
1 large egg
1½ teaspoons natural vanilla extract
Finely grated zest of 1 lemon
    (about 2 teaspoons)
½ cup milk

FROSTING

½ (8-ounce) package cream cheese,
  at room temperature
½ cup (1 stick) unsalted butter,
  at room temperature
2 tablespoons powdered sugar
1 teaspoon natural vanilla extract
⅛ teaspoon yellow food coloring
1 cup Lemon Curd (see page 220)

PREHEAT THE OVEN TO 350 DEGREES F. Line a standard cupcake pan or 12 (½-cup) capacity muffin tin with cupcake liners. Have a pastry bag fitted with a plain tip ready (see page 000); set aside.

TO PREPARE THE BATTER, in a mixing bowl, combine the flour, baking powder, and salt; set aside. Put the butter and sugar in the bowl of a standing electric mixer fitted with a paddle attachment, or use a hand-held electric beater. Beat on medium speed until light and fluffy, about 2 minutes. Scrape down the sides of the bowl. Add the egg, vanilla, and zest, beating well to incorporate.

TURN THE MIXER TO LOW SPEED and slowly add the dry ingredients and the milk to the creamed butter and sugar mixture in 2 additions, beating to well combine.

POUR THE BATTER INTO THE PREPARED PAN; the molds should be two-thirds full. Tap the pan a few times firmly on the countertop to level and knock out any air bubbles.

PLACE THE PAN on the middle rack of the oven and bake for 20 to 25 minutes, until the cupcakes are springy and fairly firm to the touch. Cool for about 10 minutes. Loosen the cupcakes from the sides of the pan by running a thin metal spatula around the edges. Turn them out onto a wire rack to cool.

TO PREPARE THE FROSTING, put the cream cheese and butter in the bowl of a standing electric mixer fitted with a paddle attachment, or use a handheld electric beater. Beat on medium speed until very smooth and lump-free, about 2 minutes. Stop the machine periodically to scrape off the paddle and the sides of the bowl. While beating, gradually sprinkle in the powdered sugar until light and fluffy, about 3 minutes. Add the vanilla and food coloring; continue to mix until combined.

PIPE A RING OF THE FROSTING around the outer edge of the cooled cupcakes and dollop a tablespoon of lemon curd in the center.

CARROT CUPCAKES

MAKES 1 DOZEN STANDARD-SIZE CUPCAKES OR 16 MINI CUPCAKES

The natural sweetness of carrot cake never goes out of style and one bite will tell you why. Embracing the cupcake craze, these single-serving Carrot Cupcakes are unforgettably moist, but the addition of coconut, pineapple, pecans, and raisins, are what makes this classic American dessert taste just a bit tropical Angeleno. Covered with a tangy and sweet cream cheese frosting, serve at a kid's Halloween party or Thanksgiving dinner.

BATTER
1½ cups all-purpose flour
1 teaspoon baking soda
1½ teaspoons baking powder
1 teaspoon ground cinnamon
½ teaspoon salt
2 large eggs
¼ cup vegetable oil
1 cup sugar
¾ teaspoon natural vanilla extract
½ cup canned crushed pineapple in juice, drained
3 peeled and grated carrots, (about 2 cups), pressed with paper towel to remove moisture
¼ cup chopped pecans, untoasted
¼ cup shredded sweetened coconut, untoasted
¼ cup golden raisins

ALMOND CRUNCH
½ cup sliced almonds, raw and unsalted
1 tablespoon honey

PREHEAT THE OVEN TO 350 DEGREES F. Line a standard cupcake pan or 12 (½-cup) capacity muffin tin with cupcake liners; set aside.

TO PREPARE THE BATTER, in a mixing bowl, combine the flour, baking powder, baking soda, cinnamon, and salt.

IN ANOTHER MIXING BOWL, whisk the eggs, oil, sugar, and vanilla until combined. Using a rubber spatula, fold in the pineapple, grated carrots, pecans, coconut, and raisins. Slowly add the dry ingredients to the carrot mixture in 2 additions, beating to well combine.

POUR THE BATTER INTO THE PREPARED PAN; the molds should be two-thirds full. Tap the pan a few times firmly on the counter top to level and knock out any air bubbles.

Place the pan on the middle rack of the oven and bake for 20 to 25 minutes, until the cupcakes are springy and fairly firm to the touch. Cool for about 10 minutes. Loosen the cupcakes from the sides of the pan by running a thin metal spatula around the edges. Turn them out onto a wire rack to cool.

TO PREPARE THE ALMOND CRUNCH, combine the almonds and honey in a bowl. Lay the nuts out on a small pan. Bake for 8 to 10 minutes until solid. Let cool and then coarsely chop.

FROSTING
½ (8-ounce) package cream cheese,
   at room temperature
½ cup (1 stick) unsalted butter,
   at room temperature
¼ cup powdered sugar
2 teaspoons natural vanilla extract

TO PREPARE THE FROSTING, put the cream cheese and butter in the bowl of a standing electric mixer fitted with a paddle attachment, or use a handheld electric beater. Beat on medium speed until very smooth and lump-free, about 2 minutes. Stop the machine periodically to scrape off the paddle and the sides of the bowl. While beating, gradually sprinkle in the powdered sugar until light and fluffy, about 3 minutes. Add the vanilla and continue to mix until combined.

FROST THE COOLED CUPCAKES with a small spatula and sprinkle the tops with almond crunch.

MOCHA CUPCAKES

MAKES 1 DOZEN STANDARD-SIZE CUPCAKES OR 16 MINI

LEMONADE flanks the corner of Abbot Kinney and Venice Boulevards, in the heart of the bohemian scene. Doubling as a caffeine kick and sugar rush, these rich, Mocha Cupcakes keep the local hipsters happy.

BATTER

1½ cups all-purpose flour
1½ teaspoons baking powder
¼ teaspoon salt
1 teaspoon unsweetened cocoa
   powder
½ cup (1 stick) unsalted butter,
   at room temperature
1 cup sugar
1 large egg
1 teaspoon natural coffee extract
½ teaspoon natural vanilla extract
½ cup milk
½ cup finely chopped semi-sweet
   chocolate, plus ½ cup for topping

FROSTING

½ (8-ounce) package cream cheese,
   at room temperature
½ cup (1 stick) unsalted butter,
   at room temperature
2 tablespoons powdered sugar
1 teaspoon natural coffee extract
½ teaspoon natural vanilla extract

PREHEAT THE OVEN TO 350 DEGREES F. Line a cupcake pan or a 12 (½-cup) muffin pan with cupcake liners; set aside.

TO PREPARE THE BATTER, in a mixing bowl, combine the flour, baking powder, salt, and cocoa; set aside. Put the butter and sugar in the bowl of a standing electric mixer fitted with a paddle attachment, or use a handheld electric beater. Beat on medium speed until fluffy and light, about 3 minutes. Scrape down the sides of the bowl. Add the egg, coffee and vanilla extracts, beating well to incorporate.

TURN THE MIXER TO LOW and add the dry ingredients and the milk to the creamed butter and sugar in 2 additions, beating well to combine. Using a rubber spatula, fold in the chocolate.

POUR THE BATTER INTO THE PREPARED PAN; the molds should be two-thirds full. Tap the pan a few times firmly on the counter top to level and knock out any air bubbles. Place the pan on the middle rack of the oven and bake for 20 to 25 minutes, until the cupcakes are springy and fairly firm to the touch. Cool for about 10 minutes. Loosen the cupcakes from the sides of the pan and turn them out onto a wire rack to cool.

TO PREPARE THE FROSTING, put the cream cheese and butter in the bowl of a standing electric mixer fitted with a paddle attachment, or use a handheld electric beater. Beat on medium speed until very smooth, about 2 minutes. Stop periodically to scrape off the paddle and the sides of the bowl. While beating, gradually sprinkle in the powdered sugar until light and fluffy, about 3 minutes. Add the coffee and vanilla extracts to mix until combined.

FROST THE COOLED CUPCAKES with a small spatula and sprinkle the tops with chopped chocolate.

BLACK BOTTOM
CHEESECAKE BROWNIES

MAKES 16 (3-INCH) BROWNIES

These decadent Black Bottom Cheesecake Brownies are a perfect way to enjoy both a brownie and cheesecake at the same time. The brownie is intensely chocolate, and the cream cheese provides a rich, tangy contrast.

BROWNIE

½ cup (1 stick) unsalted butter, cut in chunks

8 ounces unsweetened chocolate, chopped

1½ cups sugar

2 teaspoons natural vanilla extract

2 large eggs

1 cup all-purpose flour

1 teaspoon baking powder

½ teaspoon salt

CHEESECAKE

2 (8-ounce) packages cream cheese, at room temperature

2 tablespoons unsalted butter, at room temperature

1 large egg

½ cup sugar

½ teaspoon natural vanilla extract

¾ cup semisweet chocolate chips, for topping

PREHEAT THE OVEN TO 350 DEGREES F. Grease a 13-by-9-inch baking pan; set aside.

TO PREPARE THE BROWNIE LAYER, create a double boiler. Bring a pot of water to a simmer over medium-low heat. Combine the butter and unsweetened chocolate in a metal or glass heat-resistant bowl and set over the simmering water, without letting the bottom touch. Stir until melted and smooth. Remove from the heat. Whisk in the sugar and vanilla. Add the eggs, beat well. Whisk in the flour, baking powder, and salt. Stir vigorously until the batter is smooth and well blended, about 1 minute.

RESERVE HALF OF THE BROWNIE BATTER AND SET ASIDE the top layer. Pour the remaining batter onto the bottom of the prepared pan and spread evenly with a rubber spatula. Set the pan in the refrigerator while preparing the cheesecake layer.

TO PREPARE THE CHEESECAKE LAYER, put the cream cheese, butter, and egg in the bowl of a standing electric mixer fitted with a paddle attachment, or use a hand-held electric beater. Beat on medium speed until very smooth and lump-free, about 2 minutes. While beating, gradually sprinkle in the sugar until fully incorporated. Add the vanilla; continue to mix until combined.

Spread the cream cheese filling evenly over the brownie layer. Scatter the chocolate chips on top. Spread the reserved brownie batter over the top of the chips and cream cheese filling, spreading evenly with a rubber spatula.

BAKE UNTIL THE BROWNIES ARE FIRM TO THE TOUCH and edges start pulling away from sides of pan, 40 to 45 minutes. Cool completely in the pan. Run a thin knife around edges of pan to loosen. Cut into 3-inch bars.

BUTTERSCOTCH BLONDIES

MAKES 24 (2-INCH) BARS

Chewy and golden, these Butterscotch Blondies come fully loaded with white chocolate, pecans, raisins, and coconut set in a buttery bar cookie. You really can't go wrong with whatever is on-hand in the cupboard and this recipe is super adaptable—customize ingredients anywhere from creating a cranberry-almond bar to a peanut butter-n-mashed banana delight!

Nonstick cooking spray, for coating the pan
2 cups all-purpose flour
1 teaspoon baking powder
¼ teaspoon baking soda
1 teaspoon kosher salt
¾ cup (1½ sticks) unsalted butter, cut into chunks
1 cup dark brown sugar, loosely packed
½ cup granulated sugar
2 large eggs
½ cup white chocolate chips
½ cup pecans, toasted and coarsely chopped (see page 3)
½ cup golden raisins
½ cup shredded sweetened coconut, toasted

PREHEAT THE OVEN TO 350 DEGREES F. Spray the bottom and sides of a 13-by-9-inch baking dish with nonstick cooking spray; set aside.

IN A MIXING BOWL, sift together the flour, baking powder, baking soda, and salt; set aside.

PUT A SMALL POT OVER MEDIUM HEAT and add the butter cubes. Swirl the pot around as the butter melts and foams. Cook the butter gently for 5 minutes until it is a brown amber color and smells nutty. Add the brown and granulated sugars. Stir to combine and incorporate fully. Remove from the heat and pour into a clean bowl. Mix in the eggs.

USING A RUBBER SPATULA, fold the dry ingredients into the egg mixture until just combined; do not over-mix. Fold in the chocolate chips, pecans, raisins, and coconut. Pour the batter into the prepared pan, smoothing the top with the spatula.

BAKE UNTIL THE TOP IS LIGHT GOLDEN BROWN, slightly firm to the touch, and edges start pulling away from sides of pan, 25 to 30 minutes. Cool completely in pan on a rack. Run a thin knife around edges of pan to loosen. Cut into 2-inch bars.

FIG BARS

MAKES 1 DOZEN (2 BY 3-INCH) BARS

Just like the store-bought versions but without all the preservatives, these Fig Bars are simple, wholesome, and plain old delicious. The soft cookie is wrapped around a chewy figgy center; the two almost hug each other in comfort as they bake into a near replica of the original. These are my wife Heidi's favorite and a sneaky way to get a little fiber in your diet!

FILLING
8 ounces dried figs, stemmed and
    coarsely chopped (about 2 cups)
2 cups water
¼ cup granulated sugar
Juice and finely grated zest of
    1 orange or lemon
¼ teaspoon salt

DOUGH
1¼ cups all-purpose flour, plus more
    for dusting
½ teaspoon baking powder
¼ teaspoon salt
⅛ teaspoon ground cinnamon
¼ cup (½ stick) unsalted butter,
    at room temperature
½ cup light brown sugar, loosely
    packed
1 large egg
1 tablespoon heavy cream

TO PREPARE THE FIG FILLING, combine the chopped figs, 1 cup of the water, sugar, lemon juice and zest, and salt in a pot over medium heat. Simmer, covered, for 20 minutes, until the figs are soft and swollen but there should still be some liquid left in the pot. Transfer the fig mixture, along with the liquid, to a food processor, add the remaining 1 cup water, and puree until smooth.

TO PREPARE THE DOUGH, in a mixing bowl, combine the flour, baking powder, salt, and cinnamon; set aside. Put the butter and brown sugar in the bowl of a standing electric mixer fitted with a paddle attachment, or use a hand-held electric beater. Beat on medium speed until light and fluffy, about 2 minutes. Scrape down the sides of the bowl. Add the egg and heavy cream, beating well to incorporate.

TURN THE MIXER TO LOW SPEED and slowly add the dry ingredients to the creamed butter and sugar mixture in 2 additions, beating just to combine. Do not overmix or the cookie dough can become tough. Divide the dough in half, form into cylinders, wrap in plastic and refrigerate for at least 30 minutes or up to 2 days to firm up.

PREHEAT THE OVEN TO 350 DEGREES F. Grease a baking pan or line with wax or parchment paper; set aside.

REMOVE THE DOUGH FROM THE REFRIGERATOR and set it out on the counter for 5 minutes to warm up a bit, making it easier to roll out. Sprinkle the counter and a rolling pin lightly with flour.

Working with one cylinder at a time, roll the dough out into a rectangle, about ⅛-inch-thick, about the size of the baking pan (6-inches wide by 12-inches long). Continuously add flour as you roll so that the dough doesn't stick to the counter.

SPREAD HALF OF THE FIG FILLING EVENLY OVER THE DOUGH, leaving a 1-inch border on all sides. Moisten the edges of the dough with water. Fold one long side of the dough up and over the fig filling, then roll the log over itself to cover the remaining portion of dough. You'll have a 3-inch cookie log with smooth dough on top and a seam along the bottom. Carefully transfer the log to the prepared pan, seam-side down. Repeat the process with the remaining log of dough and fig filling. Put the logs side-by-side on the baking pan.

BAKE FOR ABOUT 20 MINUTES, until the top is lightly browned. Cool the logs in the pan and then transfer to a cutting board and cut crosswise into 2-by-3-inch bars.

COCONUT CAKE

Not for the calorie conscious or lactose intolerant, *Tres Leche* is one of the most luscious desserts ever invented. In this twist on the classic special-occasion cake of Mexico, one of the three "milks" is a glaze of rich, nutty coconut milk. The cake literally drinks it up, soaking the cake from the inside out, making it incredibly moist. Flaked coconut in the topping amps up the tropical flavor even further; it smells like suntan lotion in summer at the beach.

BATTER

3 cups all-purpose flour
1 teaspoon baking powder
1 teaspoon salt
1 cup (2 sticks) unsalted butter,
   at room temperature
2 cups granulated sugar
4 large eggs
1 teaspoon natural vanilla extract
1 cup evaporated milk

PREHEAT THE OVEN TO 350 DEGREES F. Line three 9-inch round cake pans with wax or parchment paper and coat lightly with nonstick cooking spray; set aside.

TO PREPARE THE BATTER, in a mixing bowl, combine the flour, baking powder, and salt; set aside. Put the butter and sugar in the bowl of a standing electric mixer fitted with a paddle attachment, or use a hand-held electric beater. Beat on medium speed until fluffy and light, about 3 minutes. Scrape down the sides of the bowl. Add the eggs and vanilla, beating well to incorporate.

TURN THE MIXER TO LOW SPEED and slowly add the dry ingredients and the evaporated milk to the creamed butter and sugar mixture in 2 additions. Beat for 1 minute after each addition to incorporate the ingredients and strengthen the cake's structure. Mix until the batter is smooth.

POUR THE BATTER INTO THE PREPARED PANS and smooth the surface with a spatula; the pans should be one-half full. Tap the pans a few times firmly on the counter top to level and knock out any air bubbles. Place the pans on the middle rack of the oven and bake for 18 to 20 minutes, or until a toothpick inserted in the center comes out clean and the cake springs back when touched. Cool the cake in the pans until completely cool, otherwise you run the risk of this extremely light cake breaking apart when you take them out. In the meantime, prepare the glaze, filling, and frosting.

(continued on next page)

GLAZE

½ cup sweetened coconut milk
¼ cup granulated sugar
1 teaspoon natural vanilla extract

FILLING

1 cup heavy cream
¾ cup granulated sugar
6 tablespoons (¾ stick) butter
2 cups shredded sweetened coconut
1 teaspoon cornstarch
1 teaspoon natural vanilla extract

FROSTING

1 (8-ounce) package cream cheese,
    at room temperature
¼ cup (½ stick) unsalted butter,
    at room temperature
1 cup powdered sugar
1 teaspoon natural vanilla extract
2 cups shredded sweetened coconut,
    for topping

TO PREPARE THE GLAZE, in a mixing bowl, stir together the coconut milk, sugar, and vanilla; set aside.

TO PREPARE THE FILLING, combine the cream, sugar, and butter in a large pot and place over low heat. Cook, stirring occasionally, until reduced and slightly thickened, about 15 minutes. Remove from the heat and mix in the coconut, cornstarch, and vanilla. Cool and then store in the refrigerator until ready to use.

TO PREPARE THE FROSTING, add the cream cheese and butter in the bowl of a standing electric mixer fitted with a paddle attachment, or use a handheld electric beater. Beat on medium speed until very smooth and lump-free, about 2 minutes. Stop the machine periodically to scrape off the paddle and the sides of the bowl. While beating, gradually sprinkle in the powdered sugar until light and fluffy, about 3 minutes. Add the vanilla and continue to mix until combined.

ONCE THE CAKES ARE COOL, turn them out from the pans and remove the paper. Trim off any uneven edges. With a pastry brush, coat all of the cake rounds with the glaze. Using a metal spatula, spread half of the coconut filling on top of two of the cake rounds. Carefully place the cakes on top of each other. Set the last layer on top. Frost the top and sides of the cake thoroughly. Generously cover the top of the cake with shredded coconut, and carefully patting on the sides. Refrigerate the cake for 45 minutes before cutting.

LEMON-POPPY SEED
BUNDT CAKE

MAKES 1 CAKE

Perfect for afternoon gatherings over coffee and cake or Sunday brunch, this Lemon Poppy Seed Bundt Cake has an irresistible taste and a timeless aesthetic. If you consider yourself a good baker but aren't the best cake decorator, a bundt pan can turn a simple cake into something truly special. Lemon glaze drizzled over top adds a punch of sweet and sour.

BATTER
Nonstick cooking spray,
    for coating the pan
3 cups cake flour, plus more
    for dusting
½ cup poppy seeds
1 teaspoon baking powder
¼ teaspoon salt
1½ cups (3 sticks) unsalted butter,
    at room temperature
2 cups granulated sugar
4 large eggs
3 tablespoons lemon zest
    (about 4 lemons)
1 cup milk or buttermilk

GLAZE
1 cup powdered sugar
¼ cup freshly squeezed lemon juice
    (about 2 lemons)

PREHEAT OVEN TO 350 DEGREES F. Coat a 10-inch (12 cup) bundt pan with nonstick cooking spray. Sprinkle the pan with a few tablespoons of flour, tapping out the excess.

TO PREPARE THE BATTER, in a mixing bowl, sift together the flour, poppy seeds, baking powder, and salt; set aside. Put the butter and sugar in the bowl of a standing electric mixer fitted with a paddle attachment, or use a hand-held electric beater. Beat on medium speed until fluffy and light, about 3 minutes. Scrape down the sides of the bowl. Add the eggs and lemon zest, beating well to incorporate.

Turn the mixer to low speed and slowly add the dry ingredients and the milk to the creamed butter and sugar mixture in 2 additions. Beat for 1 minute after each addition to incorporate the ingredients and strengthen the cake's structure. Mix until the batter is smooth.

POUR THE BATTER INTO THE PREPARED PAN and smooth the surface with a spatula; the pan should be two-thirds full. Tap the pan a few times firmly on the countertop to level and knock out any air bubbles. Place the pan on the middle rack of the oven and bake for 60 to 90 minutes, or until a toothpick inserted in the center comes out clean and the cake springs back when touched. Cool in the pan and then transfer to a wire rack.

TO PREPARE THE GLAZE, in a mixing bowl, combine the powdered sugar and lemon juice. Stir constantly until the sugar dissolves and the glaze is completely smooth. The glaze should be thick, yet pourable; add more sugar or lemon juice, as necessary, to achieve desired consistency. Pour the glaze over the cake, letting it run down the sides; let dry, about 30 minutes.

CHOCOLATE LAYER CAKE

For the chocoholic, this Chocolate Layer Cake is a memorable dessert welcome at any birthday party. This luscious Devil's Food–style cake gets wonderful moistness from sour cream in the batter. You can easily add a bit of Nutella to the frosting.

BATTER

Nonstick cooking spray, for coating
   the pans
2 cups cake flour
½ cup unsweetened cocoa powder
2¼ teaspoons baking soda
½ teaspoon salt
1 cup chopped dark chocolate
¾ cup (1½ sticks) unsalted butter,
   at room temperature
¾ cup sugar
3 large eggs
¾ cup sour cream
¾ teaspoon natural vanilla extract
¾ cup water

GANACHE FROSTING

2 cups heavy cream
2½ cups finely chopped dark
   chocolate
2 tablespoons unsalted butter,
   at room temperature

PREHEAT THE OVEN TO 350 DEGREES F. Line three 9-inch round cake pans with wax or parchment paper and coat lightly with nonstick cooking spray; set aside.

TO PREPARE THE BATTER, in a mixing bowl, combine the flour, cocoa powder, baking soda, and salt; set aside.

CREATE A DOUBLE BOILER TO MELT THE CHOCOLATE. Bring a pot of water to a simmer over medium-low heat. Put the chocolate in a metal or glass heat-resistant bowl and set over the simmering water, without letting the bottom touch. Stir until melted and smooth. Remove from the heat to cool.

PUT THE BUTTER AND SUGAR IN THE BOWL of a standing electric mixer fitted with a paddle attachment, or use a hand-held electric beater. Beat on medium speed until fluffy and light, about 2 minutes. Scrape down the sides of the bowl. Add the cooled chocolate and beat for 1 minute to incorporate. Add the eggs, vanilla, and sour cream, beating well to incorporate.

Turn the mixer to low speed and slowly add the dry ingredients and the water to the creamed butter and sugar mixture in 2 additions. Beat for 1 minute after each addition to incorporate the ingredients and strengthen the cake's structure. Mix until the batter is smooth.

POUR THE BATTER INTO THE PREPARED PANS and smooth the surface with a spatula; the pans should be one-half full. Tap the pans a few times firmly on the counter top to level and knock out any air bubbles. Place the pans on the middle rack of the oven and bake for 20 to 30 minutes, or until a toothpick inserted in the center comes out clean and the cake springs back when touched. Cool the cake in the pans until completely cool, otherwise you run the risk of this extremely light cake breaking apart when you take them out. In the meantime, prepare the frosting.

TO MAKE THE GANACHE, bring the cream to a scald in a small pot. Put the chopped chocolate and butter in a mixing bowl. Slowly add the hot cream to the chocolate in a stream and then let it sit for 1 minute. Using a rubber spatula, slowly stir until the chocolate is completely melted and smooth, about 2 minutes.

ONCE THE CAKES ARE COOL, turn them out from the pans and remove the paper. Trim off any uneven edges. With a metal spatula, spread about ½ cup of the ganache frosting on top of two of the cake rounds. Carefully place the cakes on top of each other. Set the last layer on top. Frost the top and sides of the cake thoroughly. Refrigerate the cake for 45 minutes before decorating or cutting.

RED VELVET CAKE

MAKES 1 CAKE

Red Velvet Cake is a very dramatic looking ruby-red color, sharply contrasted by a heavenly white cream cheese frosting. While the ingredients may sound odd, vinegar and cocoa powder are crucial to the batter, lending its distinctive tang and subtle chocolatey taste! This striking layer cake can be transformed into chic cupcakes, perfect for Christmas, Valentines Day, and just about any other holiday or special occasion.

BATTER
Nonstick cooking spray, for coating
   the pans
2½ cups all-purpose flour
1½ cups sugar
1 teaspoon unsweetened cocoa
   powder
1 teaspoon baking soda
1 teaspoon salt
1½ cups vegetable oil
1 cup buttermilk
2 large eggs
2 tablespoons red food coloring
1 teaspoon white vinegar
1 teaspoon natural vanilla extract

FROSTING
2 (8-ounce) packages cream cheese,
   at room temperature
1 cup (2 sticks) unsalted butter, at
   room temperature
2 cups powdered sugar
1 teaspoon natural vanilla extract

PREHEAT THE OVEN TO 350 DEGREES F. Line three 9-inch round cake pans with wax or parchment paper and coat lightly with nonstick cooking spray; set aside.

TO PREPARE THE BATTER, in a mixing bowl, sift together the flour, sugar, cocoa, baking soda, and salt; set aside. In a separate mixing bowl, whisk the oil, buttermilk, eggs, food coloring, vinegar, and vanilla until well combined. Gradually add the dry ingredients, continuing to whisk until the batter is smooth.

POUR THE BATTER into the prepared pans and smooth the surface with a spatula; the pans should be one-half full. Tap the pans a few times firmly on the counter top to level and knock out any air bubbles. Place the pans on the middle rack of the oven and bake for 18 to 20 minutes, or until a toothpick inserted in the center comes out clean and the cake springs back when touched. Cool the cake in the pans until completely cool. In the meantime, prepare the frosting.

TO PREPARE THE FROSTING, put the cream cheese and butter in the bowl of a standing electric mixer fitted with a paddle attachment, or use a hand-held electric beater. Beat on medium speed until very smooth and lump-free, about 2 minutes. Stop the machine periodically to scrape off the paddle and the sides of the bowl. While beating, gradually sprinkle in the powdered sugar until light and fluffy, about 3 minutes. Add the vanilla and continue to mix until combined.

ONCE THE CAKES ARE COOL, turn them out from the pans and remove the paper. Trim off any uneven edges. Save these crumbs for decorating the top of the cake. Using a metal spatula, spread half of the frosting on top of two of the cake rounds. Carefully place the cakes on top of each other. Set the last layer on top. Frost the top and sides of the cake thoroughly. Crumble the reserved scraps with your hands and sprinkle on the top of the cake, letting the red crumbs fall on the sides. Refrigerate the cake for 45 minutes before cutting.

LEMON MERINGUE PIE

MAKES 4 TARTS OR 1 PIE

Most would agree that there are few desserts as irresistible as Lemon Meringue Pie. The combination of a crisp pastry crust, with a lemon filling that's tart yet creamy, and finished off with billowy sweet meringue is a triple threat. These cute individual pies look so impressive and are sure to wow guests at a dinner party.

DOUGH

2 cups all-purpose flour, plus more for dusting

2 tablespoons sugar

1 teaspoon salt

¾ cup (1½ sticks) unsalted butter, cold and cut into small chunks

2 tablespoons ice water, plus more if needed

1 recipe Lemon Curd (see page 220)

1 recipe Italian Meringue (recipe follows)

TO PREPARE THE DOUGH, combine the flour, sugar, and salt in a large mixing bowl. Add the butter and mix with a pastry blender or your hands until the mixture resembles coarse crumbs. Pour in the ice water; work it in to bind the dough until it holds together without being too wet or sticky. Squeeze a small amount together, if it is crumbly, add more ice water, 1 teaspoon at a time. Form the dough into a disc and wrap in plastic wrap; refrigerate for at least 30 minutes. (Feel free to make the dough the night before if you prefer.)

PREHEAT THE OVEN TO 350 DEGREES F.

ON A LIGHTLY FLOURED SURFACE, roll the dough into a large circle about ⅛ inch thick. Place the four tart pans or a pie plate upside down on top and trim with a sharp knife, leaving about 2 inches extra dough all the way around. Lay the dough circle in the pans and gently press the crust into place, being sure to get every nook and cranny. Fold the excess dough inside to reinforce the rim. Crimp the edges.

PRICK THE BOTTOM OF THE DOUGH WITH A FORK. Put the tart pans or pie plate on a baking pan so it will be easier to move in and out of the oven. Bake the crust until it begins to brown, about 15 minutes.

REMOVE THE TART SHELLS FROM THE OVEN and fill each shell with about ½ cup of lemon curd (or use the entire batch for a whole pie). Bake until the filling forms a dome and you can see air bubbles around the edges, about 15 minutes (or 20 to 30 minutes if making an entire pie). Remove from the oven and allow to cool.

TRANSFER THE MERINGUE to a pastry bag fitted with a large, plain tip (see page 193). Swirl the meringue over the top of the pie, feel free to pipe your own patterns, making it as whimsical or as organized as you like.

JUST BEFORE SERVING, hold a kitchen torch 2-inches above the surface to brown the meringue and form a crust, or broil in the oven for 3 minutes to toast the meringue on top until golden brown.

ITALIAN MERINGUE

Unlike a simple meringue, streaming hot sugar syrup into the beating egg whites makes Italian meringue more sturdy and voluptuous. The hot sugar syrup essentially cooks the egg whites as it is incorporated, making it less likely to deflate or weep than a simple meringue. The result is shiny fluffy clouds of marshmallow. This Meringue can be used to top any dessert of your choice.

1 cup sugar
⅓ cup water
5 large egg whites, at room
    temperature

TO PREPARE THE MERINGUE, in a small pot over low heat, combine sugar and water. Swirl the pot over the burner to dissolve the sugar completely. Do not stir. Increase the heat and boil to soft-ball stage (235 to 240 degrees F). Use a candy thermometer for accuracy.

PUT THE EGG WHITES IN THE BOWL of a standing electric mixer fitted with a wire whisk attachment, or use a hand-held electric beater. Beat on medium-low speed until the egg whites are foamy. Increase the speed to medium, and beat until soft peaks form, about 2 minutes. With the mixer running, gradually pour the hot sugar syrup in a thin stream over the fluffed egg whites. Beat until the egg whites are stiff and glossy, about 4 minutes.

Makes 3 cups

PINEAPPLE
UPSIDE-DOWN CAKE

MAKES 1 CAKE

Pineapple Upside-Down Cake is a classic yellow cake baked in a seasoned cast-iron skillet instead of a cake pan. While baking, the sugar caramelizes to create a gooey topping that, when inverted, oozes down the sides, moistening every bite. Mango or sliced apples also work well here.

¼ cup (½ stick) unsalted butter

¾ cup light brown sugar, packed

1 (3-pound) fresh pineapple, skin removed, cored, and cut into ½-inch circles

1½ cups all-purpose flour

1 teaspoon baking powder

¼ teaspoon salt

½ cup (1 stick) unsalted butter, at room temperature

1 cup granulated sugar, plus 1 tablespoon

4 large eggs, separated

1 teaspoon natural vanilla extract

⅔ cup buttermilk

PUT A 10-INCH CAST-IRON SKILLET over medium heat and add the butter. When the butter is melted, stir in the brown sugar. Cook, stirring occasionally, until the mixture looks like caramel, about 5 minutes. Swirl the pan around so the caramel covers the bottom completely. Tightly fan the pineapple slices in the caramel-coated pan in concentric circles to cover the entire bottom, overlapping the slices.

PREHEAT THE OVEN TO 350 DEGREES F.

IN A MIXING BOWL, whisk together the flour, baking powder, and salt; set aside. In another bowl, cream the softened butter with an electric mixer on medium-high speed. Gradually sprinkle in 1 cup of sugar and continue beating until light and fluffy, about 3 minutes. Beat in the yolks one at a time, scraping the sides of the bowl. Add the vanilla, beating until incorporated.

REDUCE THE MIXER SPEED TO LOW and add half of the dry ingredients, mixing until just combined. Stir in the buttermilk, then add the remaining dry ingredients, until incorporated.

BEAT THE EGG WHITES IN ANOTHER BOWL with cleaned beaters until frothy. Sprinkle in the remaining tablespoon of sugar and continue to beat until the whites hold stiff peaks. Gently fold half of the beaten whites into the batter. Then, fold in the remaining whites.

POUR THE BATTER OVER THE PINEAPPLE in the cast-iron skillet and spread evenly to the edges. Place on top of a baking pan to catch any overflow and bake until the cake is golden brown and a toothpick comes out clean when inserted into the center, 45 to 50 minutes.

RUN A KNIFE AROUND THE INSIDE RIM of the pan to loosen it from the sides and make sure the cake will come out easily. Set a serving plate firmly on top of the pan and carefully flip it over.

CARAMEL-BUTTERSCOTCH PUDDING

SERVES 4

Butterscotch is one of those flavors that can make you travel back in time. This Caramel-Butterscotch Pudding is a turbocharged version of a classic childhood treat, which was often made from a powdery box mix. Silky-smooth, layered with the nutty sweetness of browned butter and caramelized sugar with hints of whisky, this sophisticated butterscotch pudding is hidden under a cap of dark, salted caramel sauce. The perfect finish to Beef Stroganoff (page 114).

PUDDING
¼ cup cornstarch
2 cups milk
3 large eggs
¼ cup (½ stick) unsalted butter
½ cup dark brown sugar, packed
½ teaspoon natural vanilla extract
1 tablespoon whiskey (optional)
½ teaspoon coarse sea salt

TOPPING
1 recipe Caramel (see page 192)
Coarse sea salt

IN A MIXING BOWL, whisk together the cornstarch with 1 cup of milk. Make sure there are no cornstarch lumps in the mixture. Add the eggs, 1 at a time, whisking thoroughly after each addition until the mixture is lump free.

IN A MEDIUM POT, melt the butter over medium heat. Stir in the sugar and cook for 5 minutes, stirring constantly, to melt the sugar. It will get grainy, form clumps, and then smooth out.

POUR THE REMAINING 1 CUP OF MILK into the pot of melted sugar. Stir constantly until the milk mixture begins to thicken and reaches just below the simmering point, about 8 minutes. While constantly whisking, slowly drizzle the egg mixture into the hot milk (do not add too quickly or the eggs will scramble). Whisk constantly, being sure the whisk touches the bottom of the pan when stirring. Whisk until the custard comes to a boil and is thick enough to coat the back of a spoon, about 5 minutes. It should be the consistency of pudding. Remove from the heat and whisk in the vanilla, whiskey (if using), and salt until completely melted and combined. Cool slightly.

POUR THE BUTTERSCOTCH PUDDING into 4-ounce dessert cups or ramekins and place a piece of plastic directly on the surface to prevent a skin from forming on top. Refrigerate until cold and firm, at least 1 hour.

BEFORE SERVING, pour about 2 tablespoons of caramel over the top of each butterscotch pudding. Store any remaining caramel in the fridge. To reuse, put the caramel in a small pot over low heat, stirring gently, to soften.

CHOCOLATE POT DE CRÈME

SERVES 6

Super silky and out-of-this-world delicious, Chocolate Pot de Crème is a grown-up version of chocolate pudding. This no-bake take on the classic French dessert could not be simpler. For best results, seek out fine-quality chocolate like Scharffenberger, Callebaut, and Guittard. Keep in mind the custard needs to chill for at least 4 hours to set up, so plan ahead.

1 cup milk
¾ cup heavy cream
1½ cups finely chopped dark chocolate
3 large eggs
½ cup sugar
Whipped cream, for serving

BRING THE MILK AND CREAM TO A SIMMER in a medium pot. Add the chopped chocolate, stirring with a rubber spatula until completely smooth. Remove from the heat.

IN A LARGE BOWL, whisk together the eggs and the sugar until well combined, about 3 minutes. Temper the eggs by gradually whisking the hot chocolate cream into the egg and sugar mixture; do not add the hot chocolate cream too quickly or the eggs will scramble.

POUR THE MIXTURE INTO SIX 4-OUNCE RAMEKINS, filling three-quarters of the way full with mixture. Pop them in the fridge to chill for at least 4 hours or preferably overnight. Top with a dollop of whipped cream before serving.

LEMON CURD

MAKES 2 CUPS

Lemon Curd is a thick and velvety custard that has a wonderful tart yet sweet vibrant flavor. Made by gently cooking a mixture of fresh lemon juice, sugar, and eggs until thickened, then adding a bit of butter to make it extra luxurious, lemon curd is a dessert staple. Divine eaten by itself, topped with berries, or spread on toast, the sunny yellow custard is also a key ingredient in Lemon Drop Cupcakes (page 196) and Lemon Meringue Pie (page 214).

3 large eggs
3 large egg yolks
¾ cup sugar
½ cup freshly squeezed lemon juice (about 4 lemons)
½ cup (1 stick) unsalted butter, cut into chunks and at room temperature

TO PREPARE THE LEMON CURD, create a double boiler. Bring a pot of water to a simmer over medium-low heat. Combine the eggs, yolks, and sugar in a metal or glass heat-resistant bowl and whisk to combine. Set the bowl over the simmering water, without letting the bottom touch the water, and continue to whisk. Once the mixture warms up, stir in the lemon juice. Whisk the lemon curd every few minutes, until it's very thick and yellow, about 10 minutes. The curd should pile up on itself. Don't let it boil.

REMOVE THE BOWL FROM THE HEAT and whisk in the butter, a couple of chunks at a time, until melted. It's best to strain the lemon curd through a fine-mesh sieve to remove any pulp and make the custard smooth.

POUR THE LEMON CURD INTO DESSERT CUPS and place a piece of plastic directly on the surface of the curd to prevent a skin from forming on top. Refrigerate until cold and firm, at least 2 hours.

PASSION FRUIT PAVLOVA

SERVES 6

These individual Passion Fruit Pavlovas, or nests, are a wonderful way to practice portion control. The crisp baked meringue base can be topped with anything from ice cream to fresh berries.

Nonstick cooking spray
Italian Meringue (see page 215)

PASSION FRUIT CURD
3 large eggs
3 large egg yolks
¾ cup sugar
½ cup passion fruit juice, nectar, or puree
½ cup (1 stick) unsalted butter, cut into chunks and at room temperature

PREHEAT THE OVEN TO 250 DEGREES F. Line a baking pan with wax or parchment paper and coat lightly with nonstick cooking spray; set aside.

PREPARE THE MERINGUE as directed in the recipe on page 215. If you want to get fancy, put the meringue into a pastry bag with a plain tip (see page 193), otherwise make the nests with a serving spoon. To makes nests, spoon the meringue into 6 equal mounds on the prepared pan. With back of the spoon, spread each mound into 3-inch round and make a well in center of each to form the nest. Alternatively, pipe the meringue into 3-inch circles on the pan, starting in the center of each and working out in a circular pattern; each island should be solid.

BAKE FOR 1 HOUR. Turn off the heat and leave the meringues in the oven to cool and completely dry out, at least 2 hours. Meringues are ready when the surface is dry to the touch and can be removed cleanly off the paper. Store at room temperature in an airtight container to keep them crisp. While the meringues are baking and cooling, prepare the curd.

TO PREPARE THE PASSION FRUIT CURD, create a double boiler. Bring a pot of water to a simmer over medium-low heat. Combine the eggs, yolks, and sugar in a metal or glass heat-resistant bowl and whisk to combine. Set the bowl over the simmering water, without letting the bottom touch the water, and continue to whisk. Once the mixture warms up, stir in the passion fruit juice. Whisk the curd every few minutes, until it's very thick, about 10 minutes. The curd should pile up on itself. Don't let it boil.

REMOVE THE BOWL FROM THE HEAT and whisk in the butter, a couple of chunks at a time, until melted. It's best to strain the curd through a fine-mesh sieve to make the custard smooth. Chill the passion fruit curd before filling the meringue nests.

lemonade

lemonade

lemonadela.com

Eco-Friendly Packaging

LEMONADE

LEMONADE IS A SYMBOL OF TART REFRESHMENT; its color and fragrance invigorate our spirits before we even taste it. LEMONADE shares the same nostalgia for a simpler time; symbolic of a *laissez-faire* sunny California lifestyle, the sweet-and-sour flavor combines playfulness with something that is generally mainstream.

Inspired by the Mexican cart vendors on the streets of downtown selling an assortment of fresh cold beverages called a*qua frescas*, this glorious array of colorful drinks are made from whatever fresh fruits are in season. Blended with water and sugar, our lemonade's rainbow hues include pink (*watermelon, rosemary*), green (*cucumber, mint*), and amber (*peach, ginger*), these drinks counterbalance the California heat.

Lemons, like salt, bring out the flavor. Lemon tastes good with almost everything and marries well with all sorts of herbs and spices, berries, and other fruits. Sweet and sour, lemons are born to contrast and balance.

OLD-FASHIONED

MAKES 2 QUARTS

Citrus is an iconic part of California life. Up and down residential streets in Los Angeles, most homes boast a lemon or orange tree, the fruit so plentiful it spills over fences and onto the sidewalks. I started my first business at 9 years old, opening Alan's Lemonade Stand, charging 5 cents per glass. Back then, I used only the juice along with sugar and water. Now, I find pureeing the entire lemon—pith, seeds, zest, and all—gives the lemonade a thick and smoothie-like consistency. For an adult variation, make a Shandy using 1 part lemonade to 1 part lager beer.

3 lemons, coarsely chopped (about 3 cups)
2 cups baker's (fine) sugar
2 cups freshly squeezed lemon juice (about 10 lemons)
5 cups water
Ice, for serving

IN A BLENDER, combine the chopped lemons, sugar, and lemon juice. Pulse the lemon mixture a few times then blend on high speed for 2 minutes until the lemon chunks breakdown and become smoothie-like.

STRAIN THE LEMON PUREE through a fine-mesh sieve and into a pitcher, pressing the solids through with the back of the spoon; you should have about 3 cups of liquid. Discard the solids Pour in the water, stirring with a wooden spoon until the lemon puree fully dissolves and mixes thoroughly with the water. Serve over ice.

BLUEBERRY, MINT

Blueberries and lemon are a classic combination; the natural acid from lemon juice brightens the berries' deep flavor. Mint mellows out the sweet-and-sour essence of the lemons. Because the lemonade is all natural, the end result will be more plum colored than a deep blue hue. To transform into a colorful martini, combine with gin in a cocktail shaker.

4 cups fresh or frozen and thawed blueberries
1½ cups fresh mint, coarsely chopped
2 cups baker's (fine) sugar
2 cups freshly squeezed lemon juice (about 10 lemons)
5 cups water
Ice, for serving

IN A BLENDER, combine the blueberries, mint, sugar, and lemon juice. Pulse the blueberry mixture a few times then blend on high speed for 1 minute until the blueberries breakdown and become smoothie-like.

STRAIN THE BLUEBERRY PUREE through a fine-mesh sieve and into a pitcher, pressing the solids through with the back of the spoon; you should have about 3 cups. Pour in the water, stirring with a wooden spoon until the blueberry puree fully dissolves and mixes thoroughly with the water. Serve over ice.

CUCUMBER, MINT

2 QUARTS

One of my best things about L.A. is the countless spas that offer refreshing cucumber, mint, and lemon water in frosty glasses. Since going to the spa is an experience that does not happen too often, I decided to create Cucumber Mint lemonade. It's a lovely bright green color and smells like summer. Serve with Silver tequila for a thirst-quenching cocktail.

2 hothouse cucumbers, coarsely chopped (about 2½ cups)
1½ cups coarsely chopped fresh mint
1 cup baker's (fine) sugar
2 cups freshly squeezed lemon juice (about 10 lemons)
3 cups water
Ice, for serving

IN A BLENDER, combine the cucumbers, mint, sugar, and lemon juice. You may need to press down the mixture a little, as the blender will be pretty full. Pulse the cucumber mixture a few times then blend on high speed for 1 minute until the cucumbers breakdown and are smooth. The cucumbers are watery, so the mixture won't be too thick.

STRAIN THE CUCUMBER PUREE through a fine-mesh sieve and into a pitcher, pressing the solids through with the back of the spoon; you should have about 5 cups. Pour in the water, stirring with a wooden spoon until the cucumber puree fully dissolves and mixes thoroughly with the water. Serve over ice.

CANTALOUPE, SAGE

MAKES 2 QUARTS

Cantaloupe has a sweet, bright flavor that can be particularly refreshing in the summer months because it has a cooling effect on the body. The flavor is also subtle enough that it blends well with sage's strong, aromatic aroma. For an al fresco dinner party, serve with a float of *Briottet* melon liqueur.

1 (3-pound) cantaloupe, peeled, seeded, and coarsely chopped (about 5 cups)

¾ cup fresh sage leaves, coarsely chopped

1 cup baker's (fine) sugar

2½ cups freshly squeezed lemon juice (about 15 lemons)

3 cups water

Ice, for serving

IN A BLENDER, combine the cantaloupe, sage, sugar, and lemon juice. You may need to press down the mixture a little, as the blender will be pretty full. Pulse the cantaloupe mixture a few times then blend on high speed for 2 minutes until the cantaloupe breaks down and is smooth. The cantaloupe is watery, so the mix won't be too thick.

STRAIN THE CANTALOUPE PUREE through a fine-mesh sieve and into a pitcher, pressing the solids through with the back of the spoon; you should have about 5 cups. Pour in the water, stirring with a wooden spoon until the cantaloupe puree fully dissolves and mixes thoroughly with the water. Serve over ice.

PEACH, GINGER

One of our most popular combinations, sweet peaches and spicy ginger add a mellow roundness to traditional lemonade for a refreshing summertime beverage. Use the Peach Ginger Lemonade to top off a glass of champagne for a California take on the Italian Bellini. Note: The peach puree is very thick, so it takes a little extra time to strain.

4 cups chopped fresh or frozen and thawed peaches
½ pound fresh ginger, peeled and coarsely chopped (1 large hand)
1½ cups baker's (fine) sugar
2 cups freshly squeezed lemon juice (about 10 lemons)
4 cups water
Ice, for serving

IN A BLENDER, combine the peaches, ginger, sugar, and lemon juice. You may need to press down the mixture a little, as the blender will be pretty full. Pulse the peach mixture a few times then blend on high speed for 2 minutes until the peaches breakdown and become smoothie-like.

STRAIN THE PEACH PUREE through a fine-mesh sieve and into a pitcher, pressing the solids through with the back of the spoon; you should have about 4 cups. Pour in the water, stirring with a wooden spoon until the peach puree fully dissolves and mixes thoroughly with the water. Serve over ice.

WATERMELON, ROSEMARY

MAKES 2 QUARTS

Watermelon is mostly water, so this lemonade is closer to an *aqua fresca,* which rely so much on the fruit for their juice. The rosemary is lovely and subtle; it adds depth and flower to the watermelon. You don't need too much sugar in this one, as the melon is so naturally sweet. Combine with white wine and soda water to make a watermelon Spritzer.

½ (5-pound) seedless watermelon, cut into chunks (about 4 cups)

½ cup fresh rosemary leaves, coarsely chopped

1 cup baker's (fine) sugar

2 cups freshly squeezed lemon juice (about 10 lemons)

3 cups water

Ice, for serving

IN A BLENDER, combine the watermelon, rosemary, sugar, and lemon juice. You may need to press down the mixture a little, as the blender will be pretty full. Pulse the watermelon mixture a few times then blend on high speed for 1 minute until the watermelon breaks down and is smooth. The watermelon is watery, so the mix won't be too thick.

STRAIN THE WATERMELON PUREE through a fine-mesh sieve and into a pitcher, pressing the solids through with the back of the spoon; you should have about 5 cups. Pour in the water, stirring with a wooden spoon until the watermelon puree fully dissolves and mixes thoroughly with the water. Serve over ice.

PEAR, BASIL

MAKES 2 QUARTS

It may sound like an oxymoron but this is perfect fall lemonade! A fresh, intense pear flavor with a honeyed rich taste, this beautiful celadon green lemonade gets its color from the skin of the Bartletts. Basil adds a floral fragrance. Mix with Pear Brandy, such as *Poire Williams*, for a sophisticated cocktail.

2 large Bartlett pears, coarsely
    chopped (about 3 cups)
½ cup packed fresh basil leaves
1 cup baker's (fine) sugar
2 cups freshly squeezed lemon juice
    (about 10 lemons)
4 cups water
Ice, for serving

IN A BLENDER, combine the pears, basil, sugar, and lemon juice. You may need to press down the mixture a little, as the blender will be pretty full. Pulse the pear mixture a few times then blend on high speed for 2 minutes until the pears break down and become smoothie-like.

STRAIN THE PEAR PUREE through a fine-mesh sieve and into a pitcher, pressing the solids through with the back of the spoon; you should have about 4 cups. Pour in the water, stirring with a wooden spoon until the pear puree fully dissolves and mixes thoroughly with the water. Serve over ice.

PINEAPPLE, CORIANDER

MAKES 2 QUARTS

Pineapples have exceptional juiciness and a vibrant tropical flavor that balances the tastes of sweet and tart. Coriander, or cilantro, has a piney-lemony taste that really makes this lemonade unique. This lemonade is a gorgeous chartreuse color. Add rum to make a delicious punch! Note: The pineapple puree is very thick, so it takes a little extra time to strain.

1 (3-pound) fresh pineapple, skin removed, cored, and chopped (about 3½ cups)
1 cup fresh cilantro
1½ cups baker's (fine) sugar
2 cups freshly squeezed lemon juice (about 10 lemons)
4 cups water
Ice, for serving

IN A BLENDER, combine the pineapple, cilantro, sugar, and lemon juice. You may need to press down the mixture a little, as the blender will be pretty full. Pulse the pineapple mixture a few times then blend on high speed for 2 minutes until the pineapple breaks down and becomes smoothie-like.

STRAIN THE PINEAPPLE PUREE through a fine-mesh sieve and into a pitcher, pressing the solids through with the back of the spoon; you should have about 4 cups. Pour in the water, stirring with a wooden spoon until the pineapple puree fully dissolves and mixes thoroughly with the water. Serve over ice.

KIWI, STRAWBERRY

Rose-colored, with flecks of black seeds, this lemonade is the one kids gravitate to the most. Kiwi and strawberry is a classic combo found in many desserts. This cool lemonade makes for a tart and refreshing—and visually stunning—thirst quencher. For the adults, add a splash of vanilla-flavored vodka.

4 cups fresh or frozen and thawed strawberries, coarsely chopped

4 kiwis, peeled and coarsely chopped (about 2 cups)

2 cups baker's (fine) sugar

2 cups freshly squeezed lemon juice (about 10 lemons)

3 cups water

Ice, for serving

IN A BLENDER, combine the strawberries, kiwis, sugar, and lemon juice. You may need to press down the mixture a little, as the blender will be pretty full. Pulse the strawberry-kiwi mixture a few times then blend on high speed for 2 minutes until the fruit breaks down and becomes smoothie-like.

STRAIN THE STRAWBERRY-KIWI PUREE through a fine-mesh sieve and into a pitcher, pressing the solids through with the back of the spoon; you should have about 4 cups. Pour in the water, stirring with a wooden spoon until the strawberry-kiwi puree fully dissolves and mixes thoroughly with the water. Serve over ice.

GREEN APPLE, JALAPEÑO

MAKES 2 QUARTS

The assertive flavors of this green apple–jalapeño Lemonade are so jolting, it's like natured Red Bull! Not for the faint at heat, the sweet tart apple is elevated by a kick of chili. This lemonade is the perfect base for a margarita when mixed with tequila and a salted rim.

3 medium Granny Smith apples, stemmed, halved, cored, and chopped (see page 3) (4½ cups)
1 cup fresh cilantro, coarsely chopped
½ jalapeño, stemmed and chopped
2 cups baker's (fine) sugar
2 cups freshly squeezed lemon juice (about 10 lemons)
6 cups water
Ice, for serving

IN A BLENDER, combine the apple, cilantro, jalapeño, sugar, and lemon juice. You may need to press down the mixture a little, as the blender will be pretty full. Pulse the apple mixture a few times then blend on high speed for 2 minutes until the apple breaks down and becomes smoothie-like.

STRAIN THE APPLE PUREE through a fine-mesh sieve and into a pitcher, pressing the solids through with the back of the spoon; you should have about 2 cups. Pour in the water, stirring with a wooden spoon until the pineapple puree fully dissolves and mixes thoroughly with the water. Serve over ice.

ACKNOWLEDGMENTS

From Alan:

To Heidi Dunn Jackson, my beautiful wife and business partner, for being trustingly supportive of my passion for food and the business built around it. You are willing to tell me when things don't taste right and defend me to the bitter end, even when I'm wrong. You have survived the roller coaster ride of a chef, restaurateur and business builder, feeling every bump along the way, and being the best friend any man could ever have. You are my confidant, co-founder of Lemonade, and most importantly Chief Operating Officer of our family and home, raising our most precious venture, our two daughters.

To my daughters, Adeline and Amelia, who wear their pride on their face whenever they hear the word lemonade. I thank you for waiting up at nights when I cook very late, so I can sneak into your rooms and kiss you good night. Don't ever stop calling me while I'm working, even if I'm cooking for the president.

To my co-writer and muse, JoAnn Cianciulli. Your writing is exquisite! Your ability to translate a chef's voice on to paper is what has made our book an exciting and fun read. I thank you for your dedication, friendship and guidance.

To my parents, Michael and Alana, who helped start my lifelong cookbook quest. Thank heavens you've always stood behind me in my pursuit of cooking and not becoming a lawyer.

To Ian, my friend and business partner, who has been a breath of fresh air since joining Lemonade. You are proof that you should only be in business with those that you admire, trust and like. You have helped me grow in business and as a person. Kirsten, thank you for being you, sharing Ian, and your entire family.

To Mario, my co-chef, mentor and friend since I was twenty, when we were cooking at the Bel Air Hotel, you are the best chef I know and have been important in my path to success. I will forever be grateful for the love, skill, and caring you have shown me for cooking.

To Roberto and Labrada, my other co-chefs, who are self-taught cooks, who can make just about everything. You've taught me the importance of "now" in the kitchen.

To all the people that I have cooked for; you have all allowed me to do my hobby while making a living. Not every meal was perfect; this thing called cooking is an ever evolving and improving process for me. So the early believers, and you know who you are, thank you.

To my entire team at Lemonade, for without you and your passion, Lemonade would be just an idea: Fiona, Dr. Brian Chu, Michelle, Casey, JK, et al...

To our photographer, Victoria Pearson, you can photograph a turnip and make it look good, and laugh while doing it!

To BJ, our editor, and Laura Nolan, our agent and friend, for seeing the value in our Lemonade cookbook.

Thank you to Adam, Dave, Matt, Phil, Gary, Riley, Marty, Roger, Angela, Chet, the Schwartz clan, and all the rest that have given me a hand in business.

Lastly, to those of you who eat at Lemonade! Thank you.

From JoAnn:

Loving what I do everyday is the absolute greatest joy in my life. Writing cookbooks and producing food television shows is a hybrid career that characterizes my passion for cooking in a unique way. As a result, I'm fortunate to collaborate closely with the top talent in the culinary world. One of the things I've learned from working with chefs is that there are many different ways to cook great food. I truly feel like an interpreter, taking the language of food together with the chef's philosophy behind it and joining them on the page.

This book would not have been possible without the intelligence and loyalty of my coauthor, superstar chef Alan Jackson. Alan, thank you for letting me climb inside your brilliant brain and put your full and delicious thoughts on paper. You are a great professional mentor and it's been a true joy to work with you on countless levels.

I am incredibly proud of this project. A culmination of patience, time, and hard work and a number of people gave me vital support along the way. I must give a shout-out to the talented people who contributed to this book in one way or another:

B.J. Berti and Jasmine Faustino, our skillful editors, and their remarkable team at St. Martin's Press, for producing such a beautiful book.

Angela Miller, my top-notch literary agent, for always telling it like it is andfor having the keen ability to recognize the right fit between chef and writer.

Sonya Masinovsky, for taking on recipe testing with me and for always giving her honest opinion. Your passion and precision are unsurpassed and I value ourfriendship.

My mother, Gloria, for fighting the good fight.

My Auntie Grace, for her unwavering love, encouragement, and her gracious, indefatigable spirit.

Special thanks to Adam "the Great," for always making me laugh. I miss you.

INDEX

lemonade
lemonade
lemonade
lemonadela.com
lemonadela.com
Eco-Friendly Packaging